Beyond Our Current Boundaries:

Peace Studies From Africa and the Global South

MATT MEYER

AFRICA WORLD PRESS
TRENTON | LONDON | CAPE TOWN | NAIROBI | ADDIS ABABA | ASMARA | IBADAN | NEW DELHI

AFRICA WORLD PRESS
541 West Ingham Avenue | Suite B
Trenton, New Jersey 08638

Book design: LiteBook Prepress Services
Cover Design: Ashrful Haque

Cataloging-in-Publication Data may be obtained from the Library of Congress.

ISBNs: 978-1-56902-9022 (HB)
978-1-56902-9039 (PB)

Table of Contents

Chapter 1

Bright and Backward Never! An Introduction

Violence is the breast milk we are feeding our young.... We have to change our mindsets, our behaviours, our value system. We must reinvent our relationships and re-engineer the way we relate in our families, in our schools, in our workplaces—with the spirit of Ubuntu that Archbishop Tutu taught us and exudes with every fibre of his being.

Graca Machel, Tutu International Peace Lecture, 2021[1]

The narcissism of coloniality embedded in the system demands of us to rethink the ways in which we give space for uhuru and ubuntu in the development of a decolonial feminist pedagogy. I link the narcissism of coloniality to the ma/ster/slave dialectic and show how the process of skewed recognition is connected to unrequited love, producing the unhappiness inherent in the system. [We must be] about

1 Machel, Graca. 2021. https://www.dailymaverick.co.za/article/2021-10-07-violence-is-the-breast-milk-we-are-feeding-our-young-says-graca-machel-railing-against-gbv/

> *inserting narratives of marginality against epistemicides, highlighting the ways in which the system co-opts us into rectifying itself and how through uhuru and ubuntu we are able to push back against internalized oppression. . . [We must] rely on new imaginaries for ways of being/uhuru that foster a respect for the Earth and all that inhabit it.*
>
> **Nadira Omarjee, We Belong to the Earth, 2023**[2]

As the world spins ferociously into the second quarter of the 21st century, anyone paying even a little attention should note that movements for social change are experiencing a bright and bubbling intensity. Creative energies seem to fire up campus protests, cultural challenges, economic alternatives, and breaks with apparently outdated ways of looking at and acting toward the world around us. The changes that these new and renewed movements represent, to be sure, are not all positive or progressive. Religious fundamentalisms, highly militarized authoritarians, right-wing libertines bent on fashioning leaner, meaner forms of capitalism, and of course fascist and neofascist tendencies seem to compete with great fervor for the hearts and minds of "we the people" yearning for better living conditions. The forces of reaction and repression do battle with science itself, as militant climate crisis activists push for greater support from the public that is told, on the other hand, that there is nothing to worry about at all. The world is in a tumultuous epoch unseen for at least a generation.

---

2 Omarjee, Nadira. 2023. ***We Belong to the Earth: Towards a Decolonial Feminist Pedagogy Rooted in Uhuru and Ubuntu***. Bamenda: Langa Research and Publishing Common Initiative Group.

So much commentary on what are essentially global trends nevertheless come from US- and Eurocentric sources. Even well-meaning progressives seeking to describe patterns or prescribe methods for analyzing and building more effective movements rely on too-familiar dominant voices, "experts," methodologies, and references that are too narrowly Eurocentric in origin or scope. The cycle of domination continues, as who we cite and what we build connect in institutions and campaigns still rife with white supremacy and colonial mentalities. It is surely correct that the 21st-century overt genocides in Palestine, Sudan, Congo, and more slow-motion genocides among Black, Brown, in Indigenous peoples throughout the USA, France, and all the neo-colonies and still-existing occupied territories around the world are US/Eurocentric in origin. The technological advances that have brought communication, partnerships, and individual people closer together are also a cause of our terrifying headlines. From pagers and electronic devices blowing up in civilians' faces in Lebanon and Syria, to drone-directed airstrikes and the threat of nuclear warfare, US governmental director of cybersecurity and infrastructure Jen Easterly confirms that the world is now "highly digitized, highly interdependent, highly connected, and highly vulnerable."[3]

The iconic mobilizing and organizing call "Forward Ever, Backward Never" of Grenada's New Jewel Movement and their peaceful revolution continues to inspire. But the 2024 electoral campaign slogan "we're not going back," suggesting that the Global North electoral candidates involved are at the center of some positive signs of hope, change, and moving forward, could

---

3 NYTimes, September 25, 2024, https://www.nytimes.com/2024/09/25/briefing/crowdstrike-technology-security.html/

not be further from the truth. The hundreds of millions of US dollars spent on convincing the world otherwise could be used to build for grassroots service improvements at least, while bipartisan and multilateral support in the North for genocidal policies could, in many instances, be ended with the stroke of a pen and unilateral policy decisions for ceasefire, disarmament, and sustainable development. Instead, the real hope for the future comes from underfunded local and regional initiatives that are often off-the-radar of mainstream media headlines and academic attention.

Some struggle directly against "genocide in the neighborhood"— as the Argentine ***Colectivo Situaciones*** did in the 1990s[4] and so many Indigenous and oppressed peoples continue to do, where survival itself is resistance. Mexico's Zapatista movement, in its far-reaching, multifaceted, and diverse tactical forms, continues to pave the way for creative alternatives. Others build organizations based on data and studies of imagined futures, such as the broad discussions held recently in northern Sri Lanka, on how the pitfalls of Artificial Intelligence could be minimized with these new technologies applied to aid peace-making.[5] Still others raise deep questions about the nature of building new societies amidst aspects of social change that remain neglected; the challenge that, even in conscientiously advanced anticolonial struggles such as took place in Guinea-Bissau, patriarchal and militarized norms created

---

4 Colectivo Situaciones. 2023. ***Genocide in the Neighborhood: State Violence, Popular Justice, and the 'Escrache.'*** Philadelphia: Common Notions.

5 The Gate Institute. 2024. "The First Ever Asia-Pacific Peace Research Association Conference on AI Concludes Magnificently in Sri Lanka." https://thegateinstitute.org/news/the-first-ever-appra-conference-on-ai-and-peace-concludes-magnificently-in-sri-lanka/.

a nation with "emancipation without liberation" for its women.[6] Collectives such as the pioneering ***¡Otras Negras...y Feministas!*** are becoming less uncommon[7] as a new generation of women and gender nonbinary peoples are redefining the terms for revolutionary tomorrows.

Taken together, these academic, activist, multifaceted, diverse ideological, truly internationalist radical imaginations and projects are the bright and bubbling motivation behind an Africa World Press/Red Sea Press new book series. Our understanding of the centrality of Africa is not sectarian; our experiences show us that the Global South in general, and African-descendant Diasporic communities in particular—along with Indigenous partners everywhere—make up the significant basis of our analysis of hope. The conceptualization of moving "beyond our America," as pioneering Afro-Indigenous, Puerto Rican/Taino scholar Agustin Lao has written about in a recent article on connecting "Abiayala, Amefrica Ladina, and Afroamerica." In his words, these new characterizations beyond our current boundaries are necessary "to decolonize our collective imaginaries and engender modes of re-identification of self, history, and future horizons, which are key in the new wave of antisystemic movements." (BEYOND "OUR AMERICA": Abiayala, Amefrica Ladina, and Our Afroamerica

---

6 Godinho Gomes, Patricia. 2021. "Memories of Violence: Women, Resistance, and Identity Construction in Guinea-Bissau." In Federici, S., Mason-Deese, L., and Draper, S. (eds.). ***Femicide and Global Accumulation: Frontline Struggles to Resist the Violence of Patriarchy and Capitalism***. Philadelphia: Common Notions.

7 See Federici, S., Mason-Deese, L., and Draper, S. (eds.). ***Femicide and Global Accumulation: Frontline Struggles to Resist the Violence of Patriarchy and Capitalism***. Philadelphia: Common Notions.

as Critical Geo-Historical Categories, November 2024, REVISTA DE CIÊNCIAS SOCIAIS - POLÍTICA & TRABALHO, PDOI: 10.22478/ufpb.1517-5901.2023v1n59.66444). This new series, to be contextualized and further explained in this brief book, aims to include all the friends, family, allies, and co-conspirators interested in looking freshly at our best possible futures based on the wisdoms of our collective history. Like the ancient Akan of West Africa, we are Sankofa birds, ready to take flight!

Chapter 2

A Burgeoning Field Matures: African Peace Studies in Context

Updated from the previously published essay, "Pan African Peace Research and Nonviolence: Dynamism and Growth Across Diverse Disciplines and Ideologies."

Any earnest attempt at reviewing the history of "African peace studies" must begin centuries ago. Searching outside the Eurocentric framework of how knowledge is based, we must understand that the oral tradition and griots of ancient times stored histories of peace, conflict resolution, and resistance richer than we can imagine. Furthermore, the storehouse of knowledge contained in the vast libraries of Alexandria, Egypt (including the Great Library and the Mouseion, predecessor of the modern "museum"), contained perspectives from the ancient world that we can only surmise, an incalculable amount of written information now lost due to decay and the design of those who would mask African contributions in European guise (Bernal, 1987). The collection and recollection of indigenous African knowledge bases and systems has been a relatively new endeavor in the academy (Owusu-Ansah, 2013), but which is now gaining significant attention and certain to increase in the years to come. This brief overview, therefore, seeks humbly to focus on the last half-century at most, when the emerging field of peace research was first finding its adherents and champions on the continent and the Diaspora.

One can hardly begin a literature review of this sort without noting that the founding fathers and mothers of the interdisciplinary field now recognized as "peace studies" were serious internationalists but almost exclusively based in Scandinavia, Western Europe, and the USA. Johan Galtung and the development of the Peace Research Institute of Norway (PRIO), widely considered the premier institution in the field both chronologically and academically, started out in 1959 with extremely limited African contact. For its first several decades, the vast majority of published works focusing on Africa in the PRIO-initiated *Journal of Peace Research* concentrated on conflict and violence on the continent, written from the point of view of Northern European scholars. Though both PRIO and Galtung's Transcend International network have undergone improvement in the current century in terms of African scholarship, direct contact, and focus of work on peace-building and civil resistance,[1] the first decades can be said to have subconsciously contributed to negative notions that have subsequently been proven false. PRIO's own recent Policy Brief on Conflict Trends in Africa, 1989-2017 (Bakken, 2018) correctly notes that despite the popular misconception that armed conflict is rampant on the continent, the "broader conflict picture" requires a "more

1 Though PRIO still has only a handful of "Global Fellows" based on the African continent, they boast connection to over 45 projects throughout each region of Africa (see https://www.prio.org/Locations/). And while Transcend's prolific Rais Neza Boneza has long bridged the organization to many key African endeavors, their much-heralded SABONA conflict-solving project takes little more than its name from the Zulu word meaning "I See You." (https://www.transcend.org/tup/index.php?book=34/)

nuanced" approach. Therefore, the orientation concerning Africa of pioneer Elise Boulding, co-founder of the *Journal of Conflict Resolution,* the International Peace Research Association (IPRA), and many UNESCO-associated peace projects, was much more than simply rhetorical. "It is time to begin learning from Africa, not just about it," Boulding wrote in 1999. Boulding was clear that an African peace studies curriculum could and should develop, through which "the possibilities of nonviolence in apparently hopeless situations will emerge."[2] (Boulding, 2015)

Conflicts involving arms, it should be noted, are not the only forms of pervasive structural violence (like poverty, oppression, and domestic violence), and certain armed liberation movements, on the other hand, have been great contributors to peace. At the opening of the 2022 African Peace Research and Education Association (AFPREA) conference in Juba, South Sudan, and the closing of the 2024 AFPREA conference in Arusha, Tanzania, there was talk of a "John Garang style of peace action." Garang, of course, was the leader of the Sudanese People's Liberation Army and a visionary actor in the development of modern Sudanese/South Sudanese politics. The founders and directors of South Sudan's Organization for Nonviolence and Development (ONAD) brought all 2022 participants to Garang's gravesite to pay homage to the hero; the staff of Tanzania's MS-TCDC led the 2024 participants to a tree that had been planted on their grounds from seeds gifted from Garang's resting place.

---

2 Full disclosure: though the citation references an elaboration by Boulding on the topic, the quote itself is from an endorsement that Elise gave to the first book of this author (Sutherland and Meyer, 2000). Her full quote reads: "It is high time to begin learning from Africa, not just about it—and this book is the vanguard of a fresh stream of writing from which a wholly new understanding of the possibilities of nonviolence in apparently hopeless situations will emerge."

Another key aspect of understanding the early development of an explicitly African "peace studies" distinct from research focusing on wars, violence, and conflict on the continent is recognizing the pioneering publishing work of Africa World Press (AWP) and its sister, Red Sea Press. Founded in 1983 as a transcontinental enterprise by Eritrean entrepreneur, political scientist, and activist Kassahun Checole, AWP has maintained offices in London, New York/New Jersey, Asmara, Addis, Accra, Cape Town, and elsewhere, surviving economic and political upheavals over the decades. Launched with the publication of Kenyan man of letters Ngugi wa Thiong'o's now-classic *Barrel of a Pen*, AWP has long included nonfiction, historical fiction, poetry, photography, art, children's books, and republication of classic texts as part of their repertoire. As part of their mission and practice, they publish as many books per year "as is feasible" (usually amounting to several dozen at least), and do not let books go out of print.

AWP has also served as a global leader in language reclamation, specializing in publishing works in African languages not usually served by other presses, and working to build markets for such indigenous language publications. Convening conferences on African linguistics and producing scholarly journals focused on regional studies, AWP has had a wide impact with well over two thousand books in print. "We've been in this business not mainly for profit," noted Checole in a rare interview, "but to make sure that our communities have knowledge of self, because knowledge of self is the most important stage before we do anything else. We can indeed do anything, we can achieve anything, but without knowing oneself and understanding your history, the level where you can reach is not going to be complete. Our mission is to make sure that our history, our politics, our social conditions are very clearly defined: the books that we write on our own." (Checole, 2008)

When Pan-African pacifist elder Bill Sutherland launched the African Nonviolence Project in 1985, it was therefore an easy decision to partner with Africa World Press. The Project (in which this author served as a junior partner) involved hosting private dialogues around the continent focused on the issues of strategies, tactics, and philosophies behind the 20th-century movements to end colonialism. The specific objective was to discuss the impacts and hidden histories of both armed struggle and nonviolent direct action in those countries most intensively engaged in the decolonization process. We worked to include a broad cross-section of key stakeholders from diverse ideological positions with a multigenerational mix. There was special attention paid to creating spaces that felt safe for frank conversation, so that even though the dialogues were being taped, those involved would feel able to speak freely and critically about the histories they helped shape.

In the end, the Africa Nonviolence Project conducted over sixty such conversations, including lengthy discussions in the homes of Julius Nyerere in Butiama, Graca Machel in Maputo, and Kenneth Kaunda in Lusaka. Meetings were held with Sam Nujoma at the Presidential Palace in Namibia, with Jerry Rawlings at the president's office in Ghana, and with Nelson Mandela, Walter Sisulu, Albertina Sisulu, and Oliver Tambo at the African National Congress offices in Johannesburg, among many others. Further meetings were set up and preliminary reports of our findings took place at conferences of the International Conscientious Objectors Movement in Ndajema, Chad, and the International Peace Research Association in Durban, South Africa. Ultimately, in 2000, *Guns and Gandhi in Africa: Pan-African Insights on Nonviolence, Armed Struggle, and Liberation* (Sutherland and Meyer, 2000) was published as an early example of uniquely African peace studies.

Directly and indirectly, *Guns and Gandhi* sparked significant attention throughout the fields of both peace research and African studies, with Harvard-affiliated Dr. Gene Sharp offering a rare nod, commenting that it was "a revealing and interesting account" allowing for attention to nonviolent options faced in revolutionary struggles. The foreword by Nobel Peace laureate Archbishop Desmond Tutu suggested that Sutherland and Meyer "have looked beyond the short-term strategies and tactics which too often divide progressive people. They have begun to develop a language which looks at the roots of our humanness, beyond our many private contradictions." At the international launch held at the New York Public Library's Schomburg Center for Research in Black Culture, then-United Nations General Assembly President Theo Ben-Gurirab of Namibia added that "the discussions and experiences contained in this book make a unique contribution to the literature on Pan Africanism, self-determination, people's empowerment, and indeed, to world peace."

The first year of the new century also saw the publication of a *Peace and Change* Special Issue on "War in Africa and an African Peace" (Meyer, 2000). The oldest professional journal in the field, *Peace and Change* was published by Wiley-Blackwell in conjunction with the Peace History Society and the Peace and Justice Studies Association (formally the Consortium on Peace Research, Education and Development). The issue brought together leading scholars based on four continents, including Laurie Nathan, then-director of the University of Cape Town's Centre for Conflict Resolution (CCR); South Centre director Yash Tandon; Committee for Academic Freedom in Africa co-founder Silvia Federici; Nasri Adam, Richard Jackson, Andrew Murray, Erin McCandless, Donna Pankhurst, and Bill Minter. That collection of scholars and activists paved the way for the two-volume Africa World Press continental survey series *Seeds of New Hope: Pan African Peace Studies for the 21st Century* (Meyer and Ndura-Ouedragogo, 2008) and *Seeds Bearing Fruit: Pan African Peace Action for the 21st Century* (Ndura, Meyer, and Atiri, 2010). Additional scholarship building on the works of Sutherland, Meyer, and the early African peace authors was championed through research and writing by Gail Presbey and in publications such as the International Center on Nonviolent Conflict's *Recovering Nonviolent History: Civil Resistance in Liberation Struggles* (Bartkowski, 2013).

With similar intent of providing space for review and production of academic contributions from Africa, the University of Peace (UoP) established an Africa Programme in Addis Ababa, Ethiopia, in 2002. The Prograssme sought to intensify scientific and experiential writing from African peace perspectives. A collection of reflections was compiled in book form in 2006, with *'Bite Not One Another': Selected Accounts of Nonviolent Struggle in Africa*, edited by Desmond George-Williams and published by UoP. The title refers to the traditional Ghanaian adinkra symbol for harmony (Bi Nka Bi), originally referred to as a possible African parallel to pacifist principles in *Guns and Gandhi* (2000). In 2008, a juried *Africa Peace and Conflict Journal* was initiated by the Programme, with consistent issues appearing for seven years (Butera, 2008). Though ultimately short-lived, the *Journal* helped pave the way for several current titles, and the Programme itself published additional important titles, all of which are made available online for free as downloadable PDFs.

Within an African context, the need for peace and justice issues to be indelibly connected has been underscored by the work of the Justice Africa initiative, producing both challenging contributions to root issues of war and conflict in the region as well as practical solution-based projects such as the Citizen's Peace Project. Founded in 1999 by four leading Pan African public intellectuals and activists from Eritrea, Nigeria, and the UK, the organization began with much dedicated focus on the war in Sudan. Early writings, such as a review of African peace agendas and the need to "demilitarize the mind" (de Waal, 2002) provided notable foundations for African peace studies in general. Justice Africa's co-founder Alex de Waal now serves as executive director of the World Peace Foundation, which has distinguished itself for its review of the constraints and opportunities of formal "peace missions" in Africa and in the confluence of "African politics and African peace."[3]

The institutionalization of Africa-based research on peace-related issues can also be traced through the development of college-based departments and programs. The oldest of these is the previously noted University of Cape Town's Centre for Conflict Resolution (CCR), founded in 1968. Though founding director Hendrik Willem van der Merwe, an Afrikaans Quaker committed to dialogue between the races, is correctly recognized as a "parent of the field of peace studies," it is also true that the early decades of the Centre were mostly focused on creating space for cross-racial/ethnic conversations exclusively within South Africa. Nonetheless, this followed van der Merwe's lifelong belief that you make peace "by talking to your enemies, not to your friends" (Muller, 2014).

Following South Africa's first democratic elections in 1994 and beginning in the postapartheid era, CCR flourished under the leadership of Laurie Nathan, a former national organizer for the End Conscription Campaign and leading anti-apartheid activist in

3 For World Peace Foundation materials on African peace, see: https://sites.tufts.edu/wpf/african-politics-african-peace-research/

the white community. While van der Merwe continued work in this period—famously helping to set up meetings between leaders of the Afrikanner community and ANC spokespeople including Mandela—the CCR itself launched the ongoing publication *Track Two* focusing on "back channel" and informal approaches to peace. In 2003, CCR's directorship passed to Adekeye Adebajo and a new Africa-wide approach was implemented. By the end of the decade, ten books were produced by the Centre, on themes relating to transitional justice, human rights, HIV/AIDS, China's involvement in Africa, and more (CCR, 2009).

The African Centre for the Constructive Resolution of Disputes (ACCORD), founded in 1992 at South Africa's University of Durban-Westville, was also critical—along with CCR—in moving from a regional to a truly continental reach in the years following the end of apartheid. Under the leadership of mediator Vasu Gounden, ACCORD's approach to peace through diplomacy has gained widespread acclaim such that ACCORD has evolved into a major conflict management advisor to the African Union and several governments throughout Africa. In addition, ACCORD publishes briefs and reports, and began, in 1999, producing the African Journal on Conflict Resolution. From the start, editor Jannie Malan noted that ACCORD's liberal approach "prefers to regard the prevalence of conflict as an absorbing and challenging reality, which should be approached frankly and constructively" (Malan, 1999). Through the years, ACCORD has occasionally partnered with groups more directly engaged in peace studies *per se* and in examining civil society resistance factors in the work of conflict prevention, and in any case have made their materials widely available and accessible for general use. One such partnership, with the Center for African Peace and Conflict Resolution (CAPCR) based at Sacramento State, California State University, in the USA, led to the convening of occasional Alternative Dispute Resolution and Peace Studies in Africa conferences (CAPCR, 2015).

Beyond South Africa, intellectual centers throughout the continent, such as the University of Ghana's prestigious Institute of African Studies, have worked on peace and conflict issues from the very beginning of the post-independence period. It was Nigeria's University of Ibadan, however, that next developed a truly consistent and serious peace studies focus, in the creation of the various peace and conflict resolution programs beginning in 1996. Their Institute for Peace and Strategic Studies (IPSS) was founded to incorporate Ibadan's various peace-related academic programs and in 2004 was the catalyst in forming Nigeria's Society for Peace Studies and Practice (SPSP), a national network of concerned scholars and practitioners (IPSS, 2016). Indeed, IPSS has led the field in publications examining peace processes both regionally and globally, in part through the development and support of numerous professional journals, including the *Ibadan Journal of Peace and Development,* the SPSP's own *Peace Studies and Practice*, and more.

Dozens of important books have emerged from IPSS authors and direct publishing efforts, including edited volumes on *Perspectives on Peace and Conflict in Africa* (Albert, 2005) and *Research Methods in Peace and Conflict Studies* (Albert, Olasehinde-Williams, and Aremu, 2014). Currently led by Tajudeen Ademole Akanji, with Nathaniel Danjibo coordinating the Peace and Conflict Unit and SPSP, the IPSS is poised to continue its continental leadership. Nigeria's University of Ilorin is also playing a central role, through its publication of the *Journal of Peace, Security and Development*, its own Centre for Peace and Strategic Studies, and its Occasional Distinguished Personality Public Lecture series.

South Africa's ongoing contributions include work at the University of KwaZulu-Natal's Centre for Civil Society, Nelson Mandela University, African Leadership Academy and University, and the Durban University of Technology, whose International Centre of Nonviolence boasts the leadership of Ela Gandhi (granddaughter of M.K. Gandhi) and Albertina Luthuli (daughter of Nobel Peace laureate Albert Luthuli), with support from academics such as Geoff Harris (ICON, 2019).

Harris is author of many vital contributions to the field, including "Studying Violence, Conflict and Peace in African Universities" (*Higher Education*, 2010) and as coeditor of the recent *Infrastructures for Peace in Sub-Saharan Africa* (Springer, 2019). Far from the falsely advertised "first book documenting the experience and potential of nonviolence in post-independence sub-Saharan Africa" as Springer incredulously and sloppily asserts, the book is a pioneering collection of new approaches for internal capacity-building in contemporary situations. One clearly limiting factor regarding internal African peace studies coordination symbolized by that quote is a lack of knowledge, research, or, most importantly coordination within the field from one region of Africa to the next. It is as if, with each new short publication or investigation, peace studies become newly "rediscovered," sometimes by those barely connected to the continent itself.[4]

---

4 Though well-intentioned and well put together, one example of this can be found in the Metta Center for Nonviolence's July 2014 special issue of "Emergence: In Focus-Nonviolence in Africa." Though editor Cecilia Lynch correctly notes that "nonviolent practices, campaigns, and theorizations in different parts of Africa have taken many forms, emerging from numerous dialectics and contradictions embedded in gendered, religious, customary and transnational histories and relationships," too much of the basis of the Metta effort centers on Gandhi and practices outside of the continent "inventing" methodology within it.

Though not always recognized by or well-networked with one another, many universities in Africa currently have peace-based centers for research, teaching, and what is often called "from the gown to the town" grassroots practice. Some of the leading institutions include Africa University in Zimbabwe, connected to the United Methodist Church; Pan African Peace University in the Democratic Republic of the Congo, based in South Kivu; Rwanda's Institute for Conflict Transformation and Peacebuilding; the National University of Rwanda's Center for Conflict Management (and its *Journal of African Conflicts and Peace Studies*); the Cairo International Center for Conflict Resolution, Peacekeeping, and Peacebuilding in Egypt; the African Institute for Development Policy, based in Malawi and including "senior knowledge translation scientist" Steve Sharra, responsible for the creation and maintenance of an active African peace educator's network; Addis Ababa University's Institute for Peace and Security Studies in Ethiopia; and the Center for Conflict, Human Rights and Peace Studies at the University of Education in Winneba, Ghana (to name a few). In addition, the African Centre for Peace and Conflict Studies, based at the world-renowned Department of Peace Studies at the University of Bradford, serves as the leading African area studies peace institute to be established in Europe or North America.

Continent-wide coordination of indigenous peace-building techniques has most significantly been attempted through the local and regional conferences and structures of the International Peace Research Association (IPRA). Under the leadership of Matt Mogekwu (2012), himself a distinguished professor and journalist who taught at universities in his native Nigeria, in Sierra Leone, South Africa, Swaziland, and the USA, IPRA has been a key networking vehicle for African professors of many academic disciplines. Mogekwu's own work on reviving traditional African communication methods (2020) helped set the basis for conversations held at gatherings as early as the 1996 IPRA global conference held in South Africa at the University of Westville. With figures such as Ambassador Francis Deng in attendance, and discussions about the exposes of the Truth and Reconciliation Commission in the air, the conference was a turning point for many emerging African scholars (Oswald-Spring, 2000).

Mogekwu and IPRA helped found the Africa Peace Research and Education Association (AFPREA), which held its first Pan African conference in Abuja, Nigeria, in 2015. Though beset by a variety of financial, technical, and logistical problems, the conference—held at the Parliament Building of the Economic Community of West African States—included substantial presentations from leaders of the African Development Bank, from the Pan African Nonviolence and Peacebuilding Network (PANPEN), and from a variety of young master's and doctoral students submitting their work for public review for the very first time (Meyer and Jain, 2018). In addition, in 2012 IPRA became the first global peace organization to elect an African as its chief officer when Ibrahim Seaga Shaw became IPRA's co-secretary general. Despite tremendous and often unfounded skepticism, Seaga Shaw led the entire IPRA network to a successful global conference held in his native Freetown, Sierra Leone, in 2016 (Meyer, 2016). Subsequently, Shaw was appointed chairman and information commissioner of Sierra Leone's Right to Access Information Commission, a crucial part of that country's growing democratic institutions (Kamara, 2018). IPRA's commitment to centering African leadership was again evidenced in the 2018 election of Kenyan activist-scholar

Christine Atieno of the South-South Network to the top position of co-secretary general.

PANPEN is just one of the African continental networks that has collaborated with IPRA, AFPREA, and African peace studies networks. Historic international peace associations, such as the secular War Resisters' International (WRI), interfaith International Fellowship of Reconciliation (IFOR), and Catholic Pax Christi International, have all enjoyed expanding relationships with African peace institutions based in the academy, at least since 1990. Following a conference held in Johannesburg at the end of 2016, the leaders of Pax Christi stated: "As we dream and work together towards an Africa that is free from violent conflicts, we are confronted with challenges both old and new that demand moral strength, innovative ideas and unbroken determination to build sustainable peace through active nonviolent approaches." (PCI, 2016). Cooperative meetings have also been held with the Network of African Human Rights Institutions.[5] A key recurring theme in many of these conferences and meetings is the essential role of African women and feminist leadership in the work ahead. At a 2018 gathering organizing in Accra with assistance from the Women's International League for Peace and Freedom, PANPEN co-convener and South African former parliamentarian Nozizwe Madlala-Routledge, serving as director of the Quaker United

---

5 Though at only preliminary stages, members of the Network (https://www.nanhri.org/nanhri-secretariat/) have discussed lines of cooperation with leaders of PANPEN, IPRA, and AFPREA, noting the need for greater communications between peace workers and human rights defenders. Security issues for both constituencies was the topic of a south-south seminar organized by PANPEN and the South American-based Service for Peace and Justice network (SERPAJ), and sponsored by IPRA, IFOR, and WRI.

Nations Office in Geneva since 2021 and the world's first pacifist deputy minister of defense, raised the cry "nothing without women!" (Hynes, 2018). It should also be no surprise that Madlala-Routledge's co-convening partner, Moses John Monday of South Sudan, is both a Ph.D. student in peace studies as well as the principal convenor of the 2022 international nonviolence festivities held in Juba that bring together pacifist organizers, organizational representatives and scholars from throughout the continent and world.

The fiscally well-endowed Carnegie Corporation of New York funded an important addition to the field of research institutions committed to grassroots realities in their creation in 2011 of the "Next Generation Social Sciences in Africa" program and the African Peacebuilding Network (APN), birthed one year later. Structurally connected to the Social Science Research Council (SSRC), the APN has become both a leading producer of and a leading funder for new research and a new generation of student-scholars, looking to connect practical, local realities on the continent with data-driven, scientifically investigated solutions (APN, 2019). Since its inception, APN has been engaged in sponsoring panels (including in conjunction with IPRA and AFPREA) and publishing working papers on the cutting edge of the field. Highly specific conflict solutions and dilemmas have been reviewed, along with more general interrogations of research-based "African solutions for African problems" (Mensa-Bonsu, 2018) and creations suitable for a just peace: "Achieving Peace, Justice, and Development in Post-Conflict Africa" (Kuwali, 2014).

The African Peacebuilding Network also provides grants to individuals engaging in or completing writing of their research, produces podcasts, and has worked in coalition to organize conferences showcasing "next generation" voices and creative, new peace-building techniques. APN and Next Generation SSRC program director Cyril Obi reflected that these efforts have brought together "both from thinkers and doers." APN's conferencing process has been able "to connect the threads from one meeting to the other," noted Obi, and "from this learning process we are connecting the local with the national, with the regional, with the global—and Africa gets to speak to and with the world" (Peacebuilding in Africa III, 2017).

In what can only now be characterized as a distinct field of African peace studies, the past ten years' growth spurt has been nothing short of phenomenal. Whole journals on one or another aspect of study have helped galvanize and concretize the field, most notably the African Conflict and Peacebuilding Review (ACPR), brought out by Indiana University Press in 2011. Casting a wide scope for as inclusive a discipline as possible, ACPR sees its role as bringing together a diverse range of theoretical, methodological, and empirical perspectives on the causes of conflicts and peace processes including, among others, cultural practices relating to conflict resolution and peacebuilding, legal and political preventative measures, and the intersection of international, regional, and local interests and conceptions with conflict and peace. In this manner, the Journal hopes to provide a much-needed "more holistic approach to the study of African conflict and peacebuilding" (Bah, et al., 2011). ACPR was joined in 2012 by another notable addition: Ubuntu-Journal of Conflict Transformation, produced by the Sabinet series of African professional journals published by Adonis and Abbey. Coeditors Ufo Okeke Uzodike and John Moolakkattu (2012) explain that their approach toward deepening African peace-making is centered on "indigenous empowerment."

That so many points of development have emerged with such gusto over such a short period of time is surely indicative of a field on the rise, including much to share with and to teach the rest of the international movement. It is thus not surprising that many authors and intellectuals have now pressed to join the bandwagon and make their own contributions to this already dynamic environment. From a detailed UNESCO report on "Promoting a culture of peace and nonviolence in Africa" (2013), to new and ongoing publications from the United Nations Institute for Disarmament Research[6] to increased collaboration potentials with African Union and governmental actors (see, for example (Ani, 2016), opportunities abound on all levels and from a vast array of perspectives. As this commentator noted at recent talks at the Universities of Ibadan and Ilorin, "Africa is the cradle of modern peace-making" (Jimoh, 2019).

With a continent so large and diverse, and sectarian splintering so deeply ingrained through a history of vicious colonialism that continues in neocolonial and recolonizing ways, it is easy, as the

---

6 See, for example: Poulton, Robin E. and Ibrahim Ag Youssouf. (1998). *A Peace of Timbuktu: Democratic Governance, Development and African Peacemaking*. Geneva: United Nations Institute for Disarmament Research-UNIDAR. And also: Sams, Katie, and Eric Berman, (2000). *Peacekeeping in Africa: Capabilities and Culpabilities.* . Geneva: United Nations Institute for Disarmament Research-UNIDAR, and the South African Institute for Security Studies. And also: Meek, Sarah and Noel Stott. (2004). *A Guide to the Destruction of Small Arms and Light Weapons: The Approach of the South African National Defence Force*. Geneva: United Nations Institute for Disarmament Research-UNIDIR, and Small Arms Survey. And also: Miller, Derek; Daniel Ladoucer and Zoe Dugal. (2006). *From Research to Road Map: Learning from the Arms for Development Initiative in Sierra Leone*. Geneva: United Nations Institute for Disarmament Research-UNIDIR.

philosophers say, to miss the forest for the trees. Put another way, with each researcher or practitioner holding on tight to only one part of the elephant, it becomes difficult at best to take a step back and recognize the enormity, power, and potential of the whole glorious beast. This brief review of just five decades of development is intended, at least, to give a history that takes a step back. Though some parts of the field described here may be more telescoped than others, and still others may be sadly under-examined, this attempt at an overview is at least one that is happily unstuck in a West Africa or a South Africa perspective, one reliant solely on resources from the Diaspora or data from Central Africa or the Horn. If we are to truly understand the power of the developing field of African peace studies, and thus the power of the continent itself, a renewed and rebuilt Pan Africanism will surely be required.

In the last words and work of the great Egyptian-born and Senegalese-bred political economist Samir Amin, the neocolonial reality in which Africa now finds itself develops only on the basis of permanent crisis. Crisis and conflict are systemically required and permanently managed by the power elites so that any short-term "resolution" will return class and other configurations comfortably to the status quo. "The barbaric violence of a colonialism of pillage and the implosion of globalized neoliberalism," Amin wrote, "have not only given rise to explosions of anger without any clear strategy, cut in the cul-de-sac of regressions, they have also opened the way to actual advances to building positive alternative strategies that offer glimmers of hope for the future" (Amin, 2019). There is hope in a field of African peace studies that delves deep into questions of justice-based nonviolence, an end to conflict because of equitably shared resources, and an end to oppression, not simply a short-term ceasefire based on the settlement of a few personal disputes.

Innovation and direct action that take these "radical" factors into account have long been the hallmarks of the approaches used by many contemporary African peacemakers and academics alike, as modeled by South Sudan's Moses Monday John, co-convener of PANPEN but also a PhD student in peace studies and a principal leader of both WRI and IFOR. Even at the center of the Sudanese civil war, Monday's approach showcases the hope inherent in this multi-disciplined, collaborative work ahead. "In the midst of growing violence, conflicts, and wars in the current century—particularly in the world's most violent regions—a novel approach to transforming violence, preventing and resolving conflicts is emerging," writes Monday. "In Africa, individuals and groups have sacrificed their resources and lives to overcoming violence and building a nonviolent, peaceful, and democratic continent" (Monday, 2018).

As academics throughout Africa and the Diaspora, or allies and supporters who believe that a "gown to the town" symbiosis is necessary to find truly strategic solutions, we would do well to understand that the period ahead will require great sacrifices of us as well. Those sacrifices, if we are to take a careful read of history, will include giving up the violent shackles of privilege and oppression based on gender, class, ethnicity, and beyond. If we are to take our place and stand true to the legacy of the ancestors and griots who came before, we will heed that call and build anew.

References

African Institute for Development Policy. (2019). Making Research Matter for Development. [Web article]. Retrieved from: https://www.afidep.org.

African Peacebuilding Network. (2019). Overview: Supporting Independent African research on peacebuilding and its integration into regional and global policy. [Web article]. Retrieved from: https://www.ssrc.org/programs/view/apn/#overview.

Africa University. (2018). Africa University's History [Web article]. Retrieved from: http://www.africau.edu/history.html.

Albert, Isaac Olawale. (2005). *Perspectives on Peace and Conflict in Africa*. Ibadan, Nigeria: Peace and Conflict Studies Programme, University of Ibadan.

Albert, Isaac Olawale; O. Olasehinde-Williams; and O. Aremu (eds.). (2014). *Research Methods in Peace and Conflict Studies*. Ibadan, Nigeria: Peace and Conflict Studies Programme, University of Ibadan.

Amin, Samir. (2019). *The Long Revolution of the Global South: Towards a New Anti-imperialist International*. New York: Monthly Review Press.

Ani, Ndubuisi Christian. (2016). African Solutions to African Problems: Assessing the African Union's Application of Endogenous Conflict Resolution Approaches. Durban: University of KwaZulu-Natal Ph.D. doctoral thesis. Retrieved from: https://pdfs.semanticscholar.org/12fa/04691d688515295a6e6de7941ef7426d6666.pdf

Bah, Abu Bakarr; Davidheiser, Mark; Hutlin, Niklas; and Hepner, Tricia R. (2011). Introduction to ACPR: African Conflict in Global Perspective. *African Conflict and Peacebuilding Review.* Indiana University Press, Vol. 1, No. 1, Spring 2011. Retrieved from: http://muse.jhu.edu/article/424025.

Bakken, I.V., and Siri Aas Rustad. (2018). Conflict Trends in Arica, 1989-2017, *Conflict Trends*, 6. Oslo, Norway: PRIO.

Bartkowski, Maciej. (2013). *Recovering Nonviolent History: Civil Resistance in Liberation Struggles.* Boulder, CO, USA: Lynne Reiner Publishers.

Bernal, M. (1987). *Black Athena: The Afroasiatic Roots of Classic Civilization*. Rutland, UK: Rutland Local History and Record Society.

Boulding, E. (2015). Building a Global Civic Culture: Education for an Interdependent World. In: Woodhouse, T.; Miall, H.; Rasbotham, O.; and Mitchell, C. 2015. *The Contemporary Conflict Resolution Reader*. Cambridge, UK: Polity Press.

Butera, Jean-Bosco. (2008). Inaugural Note. *African Peace and Conflict Journal. 1 (1), v.* See also: https://www.africa-upeace.org/index.php?option=com_content&view=featured&Itemid=101.

Cairo International Center for Conflict Resolution, Peacekeeping, and Peacebuilding. (2019). Introduction. Retrieved from: https://www.cairopeacekeeping.org/en/about-us/history.

Cecole, Kassahun. (2008). Re: 28 Publications from Africa World Press & the Red Sea Press [Web page video interview]. Retrieved from https://aalbc.com/authors/imprint.php?imprint=Africa+World+Press+%26amp%3B+The+Red+Sea+-Press.

CAPCR: Center for African Peace and Conflict Resolution, with the African Centre for the Constructive Resolution of Disputes. (2015). *Alternative Dispute Resolution and*

Peace Studies in Africa: Lessons, Prospects, and Challenges. Sacramento: ACCORD and CAPCR. Retrieved from: https://www.csus.edu/org/capcr/documents/ADR%20Conference.pdf.

Center for Conflict, Human Rights and Peace Studies. (2019). Introduction. Retrieved from: https://www.uew.edu.gh/departments/centre-conflict-human-rights-and-peace-studies-chraps.

Center for Conflict Management. (2017). The Latest News [Web article]. Retrieved from: https://www.ccm.ur.ac.rw. See also: https://scholarcommons.usf.edu/jacaps/about.html.

Centre for Conflict Resolution. (2009). Forty Years of Peacebuilding, 1968-2008 [Web article]. Retrieved from: http://www.ccr.org.za/index.php/about/history.

George-Williams, Desmond. (2006). *'Bite Not One Another': Selected Accounts of Nonviolent Struggle in Africa*. Addis Ababa, Ethiopia: University for Peace Africa Programme.

Gerbaux, Robin. (2014). *John and Elnora Ferguson Centre for African Studies*, Peace Studies Department. Retrieved from: http://www.irenees.net/bdf_fiche-acteurs-715_en.html.

Harris, Geoff. (2010). Studying Violence, Conflict and Peace in African Universities. *Higher Education*. 59: 293. https://doi.org/10.1007/s10734-009-9248-3.

Hove, Mediel, and Harris, G. (2019). *Infrastructures for Peace in Sub-Saharan Africa*. Berlin: Springer International Publishing.

Hynes, H. Patricia. (2018). African Feminists Emphasize Key to Global Peace. *Truthdig Newsletter*, September 25, 2018. [Web article]. Retrieved from: https://www.truthdig.com/articles/nothing-without-women-african-feminists-raise-the-stakes-for-global-peace.

Ibadan Journal of Peace and Development. (2012). Ibadan, Nigeria: Peace and Conflict Studies Programme, Institute of African Studies, University of Ibadan and John Archer Publishers.

Institute for Peace and Strategic Studies, University of Ibadan. (2016). Re: Peace and Conflict Studies [Web article]. Retrieved from: https://ipss.ui.edu.ng/peace-and-conflict-studies.

Institute for Peace and Security Studies. (2019). University of Addis Ababa. [Web article]. Retrieved from: http://ipss-addis.org/about/history.

International Center of Nonviolence. (2019). Mission and Vision. [Web article]. Retrieved from: http://www.icon.org.za/current/about-us/vision-and-mission-2.

Jimoh, Adekunle. (2019). "World Has Lots to Learn from Africa." *The Nation* newspaper, April 23, 2019. Retrieved online from: https://thenationonlineng.net/world-has-lots-to-learn-from-africa.

John, Moses Monday. (2018). Nonviolence: The tactics and strategies of Grassroots Social Change. In Meyer, M. and Jain, V. (eds.). *Connecting Contemporary African-Asian Peacebuilding and Nonviolence: From Satyagraha to Ujamma*. Cambridge, UK: Cambridge Scholars Publishing. 321-35.

Journal of Peace, Security and Development. (2014). Ilorin, Nigeria: Centre for Peace and Strategic Studies, University of Ilorin.

Kamara, David P. (2018). Parliament Approves Seaga Shaw as RAIC Chairman. *The Patriotic Vanguard*, November women and gender nonbinary peoples are redefining the terms forcom/freetown-parliament- approves-seaga-shaw-as-raic-chairman.

Kuwali, Dan. (2014). Just Peace: Achieving Peace, Justice, and Development in Post-Conflict Africa. *Social Science Research Council, APN Working Papers No. 2*; August 2014. Retrieved from: https://www.ssrc.org/publications/view/just-peace-achieving-peace-justice-and-development-in-post-conflict-africa.

Lynch, Cecilia. (2014). "Understanding Nonviolence Across Africa." *Emergence: In Focus-Nonviolence in Africa*, Metta Center for Nonviolence, July 2014, Retrieved from: https://mettacenter.org/wp-content/uploads/2014/emergence%20July-%20Africa%202014.pdf.

Malan, Jannie. (1999). Foreword. *African Journal on Conflict Resolution, Volume 1, No. 1*. Durban: African Centre for the Constructive Resolution of Disputes. See also: https://www.accord.org.za.

Mensa-Bonsu, Henrietta. (2018). African Solutions for African Problems: Where Is the Research? *Social Science Research Council, APN Lecture Series No. 1*; May 2018. Retrieved from: https://www.ssrc.org/publications/view/african-solutions- for-african- problems-where-is-the-research.

Meyer, Matt. (2016). Peace Studies, Historic Gatherings and Indigenous Knowledge: PJSA and IPRA in 2016. *Peace and Justice Studies Association Newsletter*. Retrieved from: https://www.peacejusticestudies.org/peace-studies-historic-gatherings-and-indigenous- knowledge-pjsa-and-ipra-2016.

Meyer, Matt. (2000). War in Africa and an African Peace, *Peace and Change* special issue, Wiley-Blackwell and the Peace History Society, Volume 25, Issue 2, 149-307.

Meyer, Matt, and Jain, Vidya (eds.). (2018). *Connecting Contemporary African-Asian Peacebuilding and Nonviolence: From Satyagraha to Ujamma*. Cambridge, UK: Cambridge Scholars Publishing.

Meyer, Matt, and Ndura-Ouedraogo, Elavie (eds.). (2008). *Seeds of New Hope: Pan African Peace Studies for the 21st Century*. Trenton, NJ, USA: Africa World Press.

Mogekwu, Matt. (2012). Going Back to Basics: Shifting Research Focus to Indigenous Knowledge Systems and Their Role in Development. In Onwumechili, Chuka, and Ndolo, I. (eds.), *Re-imagining Development Communication in Africa*. Lanham, MD, USA: Rowman and Littlefield.

Mogekwu, Matt. (2020). Mass Media and the Establishment of Peace as Path to Sustainable Development in Africa. In M'Bayo, R.; Onwumechili, C.; and Bala Musa, eds. *Communication in an Era of Global Conflicts: Principles and Strategies for 21st Century Africa*. Lanham: University Press of America.

Muller, Ampie. (2014). Re: George Mason University School for Conflict Analysis and Resolution, Parents of the Field Project [Web interview]. Retrieved from: http://activity.scar.gmu.edu/parents-of-field/ h-w-van-der-merwe-ampie-muller.

Ndura, Elavie; Meyer, M.; and Atiri, J. (eds.). (2010). *Seeds Bearing Fruit: Pan-African Peace Action for the Twenty-First Century*. Trenton, NJ, USA: Africa World Press.

Oswald-Spring, Ursula. (2000). *Peace Studies from a Global Perspective: Human Needs in a Cooperative World*. Delhi: Maadhyam Book Services.

Owusu-Ansah, Frances and Gubela Mji. (2013). African Indigenous Knowledge and Research. *African Journal of Disability*. 2. 10.4102/ajod.v2i1.30.

Pan-African Peace University. (2019). Timeline. Retrieved from: https://www.peaceinsight.org/conflicts/dr-congo/peace building- organisations/pan-african-peace-university/.

Pax Christi International. (2016). Nonviolence in Africa Conference: Statement on a Culture of Peace and Nonviolence. Johannesburg, South Africa. Retrieved from: https://www.paxchristi.net/news/nonviolence-africa-conference-statement-culture-peace-and-nonviolence/6436.

Peacebuilding in Africa III. (2017). What Next for Peacebuilding in Africa? Wilton Park Shorthand Social. [Web interview]. Retrieved from: https://social.shorthand.com/WiltonPark/jgrbTnUDZe/peacebuilding-in-africa-iii.

Peace Studies and Practice: The Journal of the Society for Peace Studies and Practice. (2013). Abuja, Nigeria: Society for Peace Studies and Practice, and John Archers Publishers.

Sutherland, B. and Meyer, Matt. (2000). *Guns and Gandhi in Africa: Pan-African Insights on Nonviolence, Armed Struggle and Liberation in Africa*. Trenton, NJ: Africa World Press.

UNESCO. (2013). Promoting a Culture of Peace and Non-Violence in Africa Through Education for Peace and Conflict Prevention. *UNESCO International Bureau of Education [12002]*. Retrieved from: https://unesdoc.unesco.org/ark:/48223/pf0000234682.

Uzodike, Ufo Okeke, and Moolakkattu, John. (2012). Towards Deepening Conflict Transformation and Peacebuilding. *Ubuntu: Journal of Conflict Transformation,* Volume 1, Issues 1-2, January 2012, 5-14. Kingsington, UK: Adonis & Abbey Publishers. Retrieved from: https://journals.co.za/content/aa_ubuntu/1/1_2/EJC128091.

de Waal, Alex. (2002). *Demilitarizing the Mind: African Agendas for Peace and Security*. Trenton, NJ: Africa World Press. See also: https://justiceafrica.org/on-going-work/

Chapter 3

Making African and Global South Peace Research Relevant and Sustainable

The ever-shifting sands mixing multidisciplinary academic fields and multitendency social movements have not been well served in written form: either the "printed word" or the arrays of mass media images and online "screen reads" that serve to document study and struggle these days. On the one hand, new books, some quite excellent, come out at rates so dizzying that reading them can get in the direct path of furthering dynamic research or much-needed direct action. That said, some texts call out for greater attention.

Though the previous chapter notes problems with the distinguished but false-claiming German publisher Springer, essentially claiming the invention of the African Peace Studies field, they have nonetheless made up for early rhetoric by publishing a series of books compiling major writings from continental authors on a variety of topics. Springer's Advances in African Economic, Social, and Political Development Series took on the publication of several titles edited by the noted global team of German researcher Egon Spiegel, Chinese UNESCO chair Liu Cheng, US peace studies elder Les Kurtz, and Tanzania Catholic academic George Mutalemwa. Together, the four produced the mammoth volume **Peace Studies for Sustainable Development in Africa: Conflicts and Peace Oriented Conflict Resolution** *(2022), an 800+-page giant that was only one of a proposed several-volume series.*

My foreword to that work serves as a Part Two of sorts to the previous chapter. It is presented here in edited form:

The hubris of empire empowers, among other things, the centeredness of various phenomena to be skewed in sometimes unrecognizable ways. Thus, debates within the interdisciplinary field of African/Africana Studies take place most fervently at conferences in the USA and Europe, while Africa-based academic interactions remain less frequent, less funded. Among the interesting discussions in the field over the past decade has been the question "Which way forward?" And while some earnest Pan-African scholar-activists have sought to answer that question in nuanced and sensitive ways, even they would agree that no answer stemming from outside of the continent itself can logically take the lead.

In Yusuf Nuruddin's fine critique of both "mechanical Marxism" and "atavistic Afrocentrism,"[1] for example, he recognizes that the nature of the academy, especially in the Global

1 Yusuf Nuruddin (2011). "Africana Studies: Which Way Forward—Marxism or Afrocentricity? Neither Mechanical Marxism nor Atavistic Afrocentrism," *Socialism and Democracy*, 25:1, 93-125, https://doi.org/10.1080/08854300.2011.576516, accessed 17 December 2021.

North, is to dichotomize where dialogue would bear sweeter fruit. Gone are the days when we had time to attend to dogmatic and rigid interpretations of the world; now is the time—in African Studies and beyond—for "harmonious healing dialogue" between the ideologies and approaches that best dissemble the ravages of white supremacy, patriarchy, and capitalism.

Is there, through these dialogues, a third way: beyond the ancient and Indigenous wisdoms of Ubuntu in the east and south of the continent or the Akan's Adinkra Sankofa and "Obinkabi/Non-fighting" symbols in West Africa? What new thinking can build beyond the 20th-century class and national liberationist methodologies that dominated both our studies and our struggles? The essays and stories, research and reports in this preliminary volume of what promises to be ongoing work help answer in the affirmative. A burgeoning field, one borne of another interdisciplinary pursuit, takes a great leap forward in this volume, helping to pave the way toward answers to questions not yet asked. African Peace Studies, including careful reviews of both effective and unsuccessful conflict resolution and mediation, relying on strong interaction between "the gown and the town," emerge as a distinctive academic discipline. As a decolonizing global peace studies pursuit insists, those in fine academic robes and gowns must make better connections to those in the towns, villages, factories, and fields where the future of peace and justice must find its footings. African Peace Studies, to which this book adds great substance and strength, becomes the 21st-century force destined to guide both African Studies and Peace Studies toward what George Mutalemwa correctly terms "a responsible coexistence of all humankind."

From the view at the global center of the International Peace Research Association (IPRA), the leading consortium of peace and conflict studies worldwide, we are well aware of another form of hubris, one I have come to term "the Scramble for African Peace Studies." In this context, well-intentioned professors almost exclusively from Europe or North America stumble upon a fine scholar from the continent boasting the cradle of civilization, and—in supporting that scholar, too lazy to look at what has come before—proclaim the birth of the new field! In fact, organized African Peace Studies has been developing in consistent published and organizational form for at least the last quarter century, recognized directly by such internationally prominent peace studies icons as Elise Boulding and Gene Sharp and enjoying the active participation of indisputable African leaders such as Mwalimu Julius Nyerere, Archbishop Desmond Tutu, and Dr. Kenneth David Kaunda.[2]

To term any singular work of the last decade as the "first" or the "only" (as some volumes from major research houses continue to do) is akin to saying that Christopher Columbus discovered a "new world" essentially uninhabited except for some uncivilized "Indians" (since India was his destination). Despite the sadness of attempted scrambles, reminding us of the 1884 Berlin Conference that resulted in the partition so central to Africa's ongoing violence and plunder, Peace Studies for Sustainable Development in Africa helps us recover, rescuing the field by centering African peace scholars in a framework where cross-border dialogue (even with those from Europe, North America, Asia, and beyond) can be done on equal and mutually respectful footings.

We must similarly be sensitive to geographic and linguistic hubris, lest a sector of the burgeoning African Peace Studies field sharply sees a piece of the puzzle without understanding the

2 Bill Sutherland and Matt Meyer, *Guns and Gandhi in Africa: Pan African Insights on Nonviolence, Armed Struggle and Liberation.* Trenton: Africa World Press, 2000.

glorious whole. It is like the story of those who focus on the trunk and proclaim the elephant one sort of creature, arguing without merit with the ear specialists or those centering their work on the feet, each only seeing their piece. Stepping back to see the whole means understanding that until we join North African Arabic and Tashelhit speaking with the sub-Saharan majority, unless we include the Horn of Africa and Amharic or Somali speakers, if we are not deeply interconnected with the Francophone, Anglophone, and Lusophone sisters and brothers, then we cannot claim to represent the entire field. Egyptian-born and Senegal-based political economist Samir Amin noted, in his preface to *A History of Africa,* that until we do better at uniting our forces and resources, at coming together as workers and peasants, academics and activists, adherents of a world working for lasting peace based on principles of justice, then "Africa will remain as it is: the underbelly of the system."[3]

As anyone who has cared to reflect on the extraordinary mineral, material, and human resource wealth based in and on the continent is well aware, the fact that Africa is not the richest and most prosperous, healthy, well-educated, and empowered continent on the planet is a lasting and gross product of colonial, neocolonial, and ongoing genocidal oppression.

But in the pages of this book and the work of its practitioner-professors, there is cause for great hope. A reading of the pages that follow begins to uncover an essential truth that we have been noting throughout the conversations taking place in African Peace Studies. Beginning with a location of African-centered

---

3 Samir Amin, Preface, in Hosea Jaffe, *A History of Africa.* London: Zed Press, 2017.

methodologies, walking us safely through the centers of contemporary conflicts and the efforts to deal with kidnappings, violence against women, the so-called Boko Haram, and others, we move happily to peace education from early childhood to university, from its relevance and "action fields" to its philosophical underpinnings. A special contribution of this collected work is its emphasis on peace activism in its own right, looking at youth and the growing significance of civil society. This proud contribution does not shy away from examining the international complexities of work with and among African peoples, and that African resources and cultures close out the book is an indication that the thoughtful editors are returning us to solid ground as we look forward to the next volume and books to come.

There is a logic to the confusion surrounding how best to center this new discipline of African Peace Studies. The steady increase of books and articles of related topics can be dizzying at times. Thus, the examination of community-based transitions found in *Building Peace from Within*[4] takes stage alongside of reflections of the history of *On Building a Social Movement*[5] and solidarity. The notable increase in resistance chronicled in *Africa Rising: Popular Protest and Political Change*[6] "competes" with the New Pan-

4 Sylvester Bongani Maphosa, Laura DeLuca, and Alphonse Keasley, eds. *Building Peace from Within: An Examination of Community-based Peacebuilding and Transitions in Africa*. Braamfontein: Africa Institute of South Africa, 2014.

5 John S. Saul, *On Building a Social Movement: The North American Campaign for Southern African Liberation Revisited*. Trenton: Africa World Press, 2017.

6 Adam Branch and Zachariah Mampilly, *Africa Rising: Popular Protest and Political Change.* London: Zed Book, 2015.

Afrikanism[7] toolkit of "beautiful trouble," while *Ripples of Hope* [8] spreads the stories of how ordinary Africans from Sierra Leone, Liberia, and Kenya resisted repression and war without the use of violence. New studies on *Reconciliation in Northern Nigeria*[9] and on *Peace Education for Violence Prevention*[10] show how African leadership and ingenuity regarding peace methods can stand up against the planned *Tomorrow's Battlefield*[11] of US proxy wars and secret operations designed by recolonizing institutions like the US African Command (AFRICOM).

There is hope in the future foundation-building of the African Peace Research and Education Association (AFPREA), IPRA's own regional association that is honored to be associated with this work and its related projects. We are proud but not surprised that AFPREA's founders have also been at the cutting edge of other efforts building toward the future of Peace Studies. AFPREA's early executive member Matt Mogekwu, for example, has long been a leader in the development of Peace Journalism, noting that in Africa and beyond, "the mass media have the greatest potential to deal with

7 Juman Abujbara, Sungu Oyoo, Phil Wilmot, and Andrew Boyd, eds. *New Pan-Afrikanism: A Toolkit for Making Beautiful Trouble.* Beautiful Trouble, 2020, https://www.beautifultrouble.org/store/p/new-pan-afrikanism-toolkit, accessed 17 December 2021.

8 Robert M. Press, *Ripples of Hope: How Ordinary People Resist Repression Without Violence.* Amsterdam: Amsterdam University Press, 2015.

9 Olufemi Oluniyi, *Reconciliation in Northern Nigeria: The Space for Public Apology.* Lagos: Frontier Press, 2016.

10 Sylvester B. Maphosa and Alphonse Keasley, eds., *Peace Education for Violence Prevention in Fragile African Societies.* Pretoria: Africa Institute of South Africa, 2016.

11 Nick Turse, *Tomorrow/s Battlefield: US Proxy Wars and Secret Ops in Africa*. Chicago: Haymarket Books, 2015.

the human mind to bring about change."[12] AFPREA's Bernedette Muthien continues to lead work in both Indigenous Peace Studies and the vital feminist/womanist peace perspectives, calling on us to rethink our concepts of Africa herself,[13] and—like Ghana's Sankofa bird—reinterpret the past to see clearly our work for the future.[14]

As African Peace Studies is emboldened by this book, the series to follow, and our overall project to bring ever-more African-based students, scholars, and our communities in contact with one another and with those non-African supporters willing to listen and support, we come ever-so closer to the sustainable peace, which the entire world so needs and deserves. Heed well the words contained herein...and join us!

Looking back on this recent but still-dated introduction and summary of currents in the field, it becomes evident that we face an urgent need for a more holistic and African-centered space to help bring together these various streams, peoples, and approaches. The creation of this African Peace series within Africa World Press and Red Sea Press emerged specifically in response to this call.

---

12 Matt Mogekwu, "Mass Media and the Establishment of Peace as Path to Sustainable Development in Africa," in Richard M'Bayo, Chuka Onwumechili, and Bala Musa, eds. *Communication in an Era of Global Conflicts: Principles and Strategies for 21st Century Africa.* Lanham: University Press of America, 2020.
13 Bernedette Muthien and Jane Bam, *Rethinking Africa: Indigenous Women Re-interpret Southern Africa's Pasts.* Auckland Park: Fanele/Jacana Media, 2021.
14 See also: Ron Singler, *Uhuru Revisited: Interviews with African Pro-Democracy Leaders.* Trenton, Africa World Press, 2015.

Chapter 4

Pan-Africanism as Progressive Panacea: Retooling the Visions of Revolutionary "Positive Action," Ujamaa, and Ubuntu

Revolutions are brought about by men (sic) who think as men of action and act as men of thought.[1]
—Kwame Nkrumah, Consciencism (1964)

As we review "the classics"—influential writings of literary and/or historic merit—from many genres and sociocultural perspectives, it is important to remember the Native American adage of many peoples of Turtle Island: that our work, like our words, should provide sustainably useful sentiments at least seven generations into the future. This "seventh generation" value[2] itself derives from the Confederacy of the Six Nations—the Haudenosaunee peoples of the northeastern Americas. But it harkens me back also to the profound Lebanese American poet-visionary Khalil Gibran,

1 Kwame Nkrumah, "*Consciencism*," Monthly Review Press, 1962, p. 23.
2 https://www.haudenosauneeconfederacy.com/values.

who reminded us that our very own "next generations" are not, in fact, "our own" at all.

Gibran wrote:

> "Your children are not your children.
> They are the sons and daughters of Life's longing for itself.
> They come through you but not from you,
> And though they are with you, yet they belong not to you.
>
> "You may give them your love but not your thoughts,
> For they have their own thoughts.
> You may house their bodies but not their souls,
> For their souls dwell in the house of tomorrow, which
> you cannot visit, not even in your dreams.
> You may strive to be like them but seek not to make
> them like you."[3]

Somehow these thoughts about the future resonate strongly as the words "classic" and "Africa" rock my 21st-century brain, trying to wrap around the words and work of the Pan African giants whose unfinished revolutions could provide roadmaps for the future of all humankind. Careful to review these works from their own historic moments in time, we can note their continued relevance—the ways in which those lived experiences of the end of the last century have come through us though not from us—while also not becoming too focused on these texts as prescriptive. Reading the words of Osagyefo Kwame Nkrumah, we can find building blocks for constructing the house of tomorrow—insightful and important so long as we use the building materials of our own century into the mix.

---

3 Khalil Gibran, "Your Children," https://poets.org/poem/children-1.

Positives and Negatives

In the seventy-five years or so since Kwame Nkrumah wrote the influential essay, "What I Mean by Positive Action," social movement theorists and historians of civil resistance alike have pointed to this key text as evidence of the leading 20th-century Pan-Africanist's interest in and possible commitment to nonviolence. Already a mature political thinker and campaigner, by 1950 Nkrumah had completed his academic studies, earning degrees in the US and at the London School of Economics. At age forty, he had returned home to the Gold Coast a committed independence activist, forming in 1949 the party that would ultimately lead his nation in becoming Ghana, the first African state to rid itself from her colonial shackles. The Convention People's Party pamphlet and later campaign extolled the virtues of earlier direct-action efforts that had taken place over the preceding decades: mass strikes and boycotts, mobilizations, and protests led by veterans, market women, and youth. As a decolonial militant with Britain as the focus of one's attention, it would have been impossible in that time period not to look to Mohandas Gandhi and the nonviolent campaigns that had just two years earlier won India her independence from the empire upon which previously "the sun never set." Thus, Positive Action helped secure Nkrumah's global status as "the Gandhi of Africa."[4]

As the interdisciplinary field of Peace Studies enters a mature phase evidenced by the development of multiple sub-fields and internal accountability critiques, the passing of visionary founder

4 Sutherland and Meyer, *Guns and Gandhi in Africa,* Africa World Press, 2000.

Johan Galtung provides an opportunity to revisit his notion of positive and negative peace—among the more important of Galtung's innovations. In summary, Galtung's formulations on violence and peace developed from the mid-1960s to 1970s, ultimately assigning a definition of negative peace as the absence of war, direct personal violence, assaults, riots, terrorism, and such. Positive peace is described as freedom from the structural violences of poverty, capitalism, and economic oppression, the causes of war including colonialism, imperialism, patriarchy, and social injustice as a whole.[5] Thus, positive peace requires the kind of resistance, decolonization, and radicalism that only certain sectors of peace studies show interest in. Liberal and neoliberal conflict resolution and mediation efforts, "war studies," anti-violence sections of the field of international relations, and social movement analysis that fails to give voice to the grassroots actors most affected by the lack of successful change may well find comfortable places in the academic lexicon of "peace studies," but they do not conform to the notions of building toward "positive peace." A decolonized peace studies, like resistance studies and emerging concepts of revolutionary nonviolence, are uniquely up to the task of imagining and building for Positive Peace. It follows that, in this construct, Kwame Nkrumah's "Positive Action" and his later work fit well into this discourse with more than just linguistic or rhetorical connections.

As Nkrumah experienced the complexities of moving from anticolonial protest and liberation movement to day-to-day governance, including management of domestic and foreign affairs, his thoughts about "positive action" evolved. In the heady early

---

5 Baljit Singh Grewal, JG: P and N Peace, https://www.buildingpeaceforum.com/no/fred/Positive_Negative_peace.pdf.

days just before and after formal Ghanaian independence, even Nkrumah's nationalist freedom dreams seemed open to internationalist compromises. On his Christmas 1957 Broadcast to the Nation, he proclaimed: "This is no time for hatred or recrimination. We in Ghana are ready to forget the past and make any compromise of our national sovereignty towards the attainment of world peace."[6] In 1960, to assist in working out concrete action plans for peace, a Conference on Positive Action and Security in Africa was convened. "We do not threaten anyone and we renounce the foul weapons that threaten the very existence of life on our planet," Nkrumah asserted in his Welcoming Address. "Rather we put our trust in the awakening consciousness of mankind which rejects this primitive barbarism and believe firmly in "positive action."[7] Over a decade after the original publication of the positive action pamphlet, and some years after becoming Ghana's head of state, Nkrumah still asserted a Pan-African worldview that was mainly focused on an antimilitarist *modus operandi*. In the preface to 1961's *I Speak of Freedom* (1961), he wrote:

> We have to prove that greatness is not to be measured in stockpiles of atom bombs. I believe strongly and sincerely that with the deep-rooted wisdom and dignity, the innate respect for human lives, the intense humanity that is our heritage, the African race, united under one federal government, will emerge not as just another world bloc to flaunt its wealth and strength, but as a Great Power

6 Kwame Nkrumah, *Axioms of Kwame Nkrumah: Freedom Fighters Edition*, PanAf Press, 2009.

7 Kwame Nkrumah, from Welcome Speech to the 7 April 1960 conference, Axioms, PanAfr Press, 2009, p.100.

> whose greatness is indestructible because it is not built on fear, envy, and suspicion, nor won at the expense of others, but founded on hope, trust, friendship and directed to the good of all mankind (sic).[8]

With the long-established principle that Ghana's independence movement preferred "self-government with danger to servitude in tranquility,"[9] Nkrumah's most dramatic ideological shifts took place after the dramatic events of early 1966: the violent coup d'etat that removed Nkrumah from state power and from his homeland for the rest of his life. Almost as dramatic, in an act of unprecedented solidarity and Pan Africanist respect for Nkrumah's leadership, the government of Sekou Toure's neighboring Guinea offered Nkrumah not simply safe refuge, but a role as co-president of the emerging, socialist, Francophone country. Toure took Nkrumah's teachings on a continent-wide United Africa seriously, adding his own Marxist-Leninist adaptations of how Africa was "on the move."[10] As notions of Black Power and Black Consciousness were sweeping the world, the chief US organizer and adherent of the new generation of militants—Stokely Carmichael,[11] with a history in both the Student Nonviolent Coordinating Committee as well as the Black Panther Party for Self-Defense moved to Africa, changed his name to Kwame Ture in deference to his two great mentors and worked to build the global All-African-Peoples-Revolutionary-Party of Nkrumah's and Toure's dreams.

---

8 Kwame Nkrumah, *I Speak of Freedom,* PanAfr Press, 2009.

9 Motto of the Accra newspaper.

10 Ahmed Sekou Toure, *Africa: On the Move,* PanAfr Press, 2010.

11 Stokely Carmichal with Ekuweme Michael Thewell, *Ready for Revolution*, Scribner, 2005; with commentary to the author by Bob Brown.

Though Nkrumah's writings during this intensely internationalist moment first focused on the "dark days in Ghana"[12]—the CIA machinations behind the coup, and on his unrealized lifelong plans to return triumphantly to his own country—he later wrote some of his most far-reaching and profound contributions. In *Neocolonialism: The Last Stage of Imperialism* (1965) and his extensive additional writings on the neocolonial condition that followed, Nkrumah laid out the basic problematic that plagues the Global South up to the current day.

Neocolonialism and 21st-Century Imperialisms

In addition to asserting the primacy of colonial and neocolonial contradictions as the major reactionary forces of the modern period, Nkrumah in this period helped usher in new radical thinking on several grounds. First, as an early proponent of the Non-Aligned Movement and the post-Bandung networks that understood the sweeping significance of the Global South (then referred to as the Third World), Nkrumah established that every revolutionary national mobilization and movement needed to be based on its own sociocultural, political realities. Thus, African wisdoms and traditional, Indigenous practices were more than tactical or theoretical additions to Nkrumahist practice, but a central part of his Pan-African principles and practice. His Ghanaian connections to existing African kings and traditional leaders might still have been in development at the time of his removal from power, but they had long played a role in his coalition approach to domestic and regional power-sharing.

12 Kwame Nkrumah, Dark Days in Ghana, PanAf Press, 2009.

In addition, Nkrumah asserted that revolutionary ideology couldn't merely refute the evils of an existing "dying" order, power structure, or oppressive system. "Revolutionary ideology," according to Nkrumah, must be built upon a "positive creative theory, the guiding light of the emerging social order."[13] His view that the "budding future is always stronger than the withering past" was based on a confidence that the long arc of history shows that we learn from and build on our previous errors and weaknesses.[14] Nkrumah's concepts of revolution were also distinctly opposed to any separation between people in struggle against capitalism, imperialism, and (neo)colonialism. His Africanist foundations did not favor the concept "Third World" as a separate force from all those fighting for socialist revolution—though he eschewed a Marxist orthodoxy that failed to take into consideration the sociopolitical roots of African or other regional struggles. Even within the popular Fanonist notions of radical psychological development, Nkrumah noted, "I do not deny the existence of the struggling 'wretched of the earth,' but maintain that they do not exist in isolation as a 'Third World,' They are an integral part of the revolutionary world and are committed to the hilt in the struggle against capitalism to end the exploitation of man by man."[15]

Even within the not uncommon socialist/anticapitalist, Pan-Africanist, and Non-Aligned framework of the 1960s, Nkrumah's conceptualizations of neocolonialism were still visionary and advanced. He stressed the trickery inherent in the hopes of the recolonizing powers who never intended to give up the lucrative

13 Kwame Nkrumah, "Consciencism," Monthly Review Press, 1964, p. 34.

14 Kwame Nkrumah, "Neocolonialism: The Last Stage of Imperialism," PanAf Press, 2009, p. 252.

15 Kwame Nkrumah, *Two Myths*, PanAf Press, 1969.

controls gained during the "scramble" for Africa and the class exploitation of the world. With a correct, anti-neocolonial (anti-colonial) ideological foundation such as Pan-Africanism, Nkrumah firmly believed that neocolonialism's "sleights of hand will constantly stand exposed."[16] Nkrumah foresaw that the covert maneuverings of men and governments required for the creation of these client states—developed "free from the stigma of political rule"[17]—would transcend individual nations and governmental parties; neocolonial subjects could be economically, militarily, and otherwise controlled by more than a single national colonial entity. Furthermore, the "cajolement, the wheedlings (sic), the seduction and the Trojan horses of neocolonialism" had an advantage over direct colonialism in their ability to entice the support of subjected peoples with "sweet music" played alongside its monstrous, subordinating, and deeply exploitative policies. Thus, from Nkrumah's perspective, "neocolonialism is the worst form of imperialism."[18]

Though the Founding Father of postcolonial Ghana, Nkrumah nevertheless saw easily through the weaknesses and limitations of nationalism. "The nationalist phase," he wrote, "is a necessary step in the liberation struggle but must never be regarded as the final solution to the problem raised by the economic and political exploitation of our people. For nationalism is narrow in its application."[19] Like Gandhi before him, an emphasis on regional cooperation expanded well beyond his national or even continental

---

16 Kwame Nkrumah, *Consciencism,* Monthly Review Press, 1964, p. 105.

17 Kwame Nkrumah, *Africa Must Unite,* PanAf Press, 2007, p. 174.

18 Kwame Nkrumah, Neocolonialism: *The Last Stage of Imperialism*, PanAf Press, 2009, Intro. p. xi.

19 Kwame Nkrumah, *Handbook of Revolutionary Warfare,* International Publishers, 1969, p. 25.

borders; Nkrumah's time in the US and UK helped sensitize him to the plight of the African Diaspora. A small but highly influential core of African Americans, some of whom emigrated to the Gold Coast long before independence, helped build lasting bridges between people of African descent. Poet Maya Angelou was surely the most well-known of these early Pan-Africanists, but World War Two conscientious objector Bill Sutherland (who married Cape Coast playwright and educator Efua, who was to become Maya's best friend) also played a significant role. Sutherland served as hospitality officer for Nkrumah's All-African Peoples' Conference, held in Accra in 1958, and organized for the Positive Action for Peace and Security conference held in the capital in April 1960. As a lifelong advocate of radical nonviolent resistance, Sutherland also served as a personal and political model of what he called "playing between the cracks": working nuanced, flexible, and pragmatic approaches toward building revolutionary freedom movements.[20]

The contemporary question of "diverse tactics" within strategic liberation movements was also something that Nkrumah wrote about. After his dispossession of power, writing *Handbook of Revolutionary Warfare* from exile in Guinea, Nkrumah certainly veered from Gandhi in his full acceptance of the necessity of armed struggle. Even here, however, Nkrumah's grasp of the importance of pragmatism and rejection of dogmatism is noteworthy. Unlike the majority of contemporary late-1960s/1970s national liberation leaders and supporters, Nkrumah maintained an understanding that engaging in armed actions was not the be-all-and-end-all for successful revolutionary movements. After the coup in Ghana and the Sharpeville Massacre in South Africa, many on the continent

20 Sutherland and Meyer, *Guns and Gandhi in Africa,* Africa World Press, 2000.

were ready to (and did) proclaim that nonviolence didn't work—that the strategies connected to nonviolent action must be rejected in favor of armed action that would win where nonviolence had failed. Nkrumah took an alternate view.

"There is no fundamental difference between armed struggle as such and revolutionary action of a civil type," he insisted. "The various methods of our struggle, and the changing from one method to another should be determined mainly by the circumstances and the set of conditions prevailing in a given territory."[21] In making these specifications, Nkrumah was in some ways, indicating that a "revolutionary nonviolence" (as now more commonly called) might exist alongside radical armed actions, both essential and both requiring deeply considered strategic analysis of a given historical circumstance, material conditions, cultural context, and more. This nondogmatic pragmatism foreshadowed current considerations and dialogues taking place among the still-directly-colonized peoples of Western Sahara, West Papua, Ambazonia, and beyond. Nkrumah prefigured the distinctions between methodology, ideology, and principled commitment to social change.

Retooling Pan-Africanism for World Peace

These distinctions are not insignificant in planning for the world situation facing peacemakers and liberationists today. The dichotomized notions infecting both the pacifist and armed struggle proponents of 21st-century social change still squabble about the centrality and predominance of their own strategic or tactical

21 Kwame Nkrumah, *Handbook of Revolutionary Warfare,* International Publishers, 1969, p. 24.

preferences while failing to listen both to one another and to those on the ground suffering and struggling for solutions beyond the rhetoric. Nonviolent activists point ahistorically to the unarmed "miracles" of the end of apartheid South Africa as armed advocates misquote Fanon out of context and suggest that armed struggle has somehow been or can be made equivalent to the ideal of successful national liberation. As some Western social scientists continue to search for more kernels of new relevancy in 100-year-old tracks of a man they unselfconsciously call the "great soul," others note more poignantly that even in modern Ghana, the civil resistance that is rooted in that country's philosophical and practical past is "relatively unknown" and "little heralded."[22] As a whole, we seem woefully unprepared to confront the dialectical challenges of our time, unwilling to even confront the nuances laden in each of these examples of half-correct analysis.

This is a time when the concept of nationalism itself is facing increasing critiques from a left that is beginning to acknowledge the experiences and voices of Indigenous peoples and nonlinear struggle, looking to build a world where many worlds may fit.[23] The half-truths of both sides of the nonviolence/violence debate cannot satisfy the quest for a holistic 21st-century strategic praxis. Yet Polisario has at times sought to look boldly at these dialectical challenges, as has the fighting feminist forces of Rojava. While frontline movements look for answers that offer more than oversimplifications, solidarity "allies" seem less up to the task of peering boldly into the future.

---

22 Gail Presbey, in Rediscovering Nonvionlent *History* (Bartkowski, ed.), Ghana: NV Resistance in the Independence Movement, 1890s-1950s.
23 John Holloway, *Change the World Without Taking Power: The Meaning of Revolution Today*, Pluto Press, 2019.

Any fast-forward to these current challenges should not by-pass African front line of years past: the initiatives centered in that "city of peace" capital of postindependence Tanzania, and the work of Mwalimu Julius Kambarage Nyerere. Similarly, in South Africa before and after the end of political apartheid, Archbishop Desmond Mpilo Tutu and the teams of people around him more often than not sought to build new organizations and initiatives beyond narrow sectarian vanguardism. Both these men extracted modern-day lessons from Indigenous African traditions. As first leader of independent Tanzania, Nyerere made sure that KiSwahili—the language of the majority of the nation's peoples—would stand alongside English as the official language taught in schools and spoken in all formal spaces. He also designed a wide-ranging African socialist program, based from a bottom-up village economic blueprint, insisting that this UJAMAA program would bring prosperity to the poor nation. Sadly, Nyerere himself understood in later years that the Ujamma of his dreams was never implemented in any serious way despite his top government position; too much wealth was to be gained in corrupt, neocolonial dealings, even in the heady days following self-rule.

Archbishop Tutu, a generation later, on the other hand, witnessed the neoliberal, militarized, and authoritarian states that had come to characterize postindependence Africa by the 1990s. Looking at the potential violent splits and ineffective political-economic initiatives of South Africa's neighbors, he promoted a now-universally-widespread notion of UBUNTU—the idea that everyone's humanity is inexorably bound up in everyone else's. This notion in many ways combines the "beloved community" conceptions of Rev. Dr. Martin Luther King, Jr., with the Islamic universalism of the mature El Hajj Malik El-Shabazz (Minister Malcolm X), both of whom were greatly admired by Tutu. To be sure, this author was a mentee of and eventually coauthor with Pan-Africanist Bill Sutherland, who helped bring MLK to the 1958 Ghanaian independence celebrations and served as guide to Malcolm on his 1964 visit to Tanzania. Sutherland was also a close friend of Desmond Tutu, who wrote the foreword to our book exploring these themes as well as two other books of mine.[24] Arch Tutu, Sutherland, and I discussed these issues—neocolonialism, violence/nonviolence, Ujamaa/Ubuntu, and the ways forward for lasting, people-based freedom. It should be no surprise that strategic thinking beyond the easy and easily unsatisfying answers was central to these discussions and that action on the side of the oppressed always took precedence over political expedient concerns.

It is also no surprise that contemporary Pan-African spaces hold close to these themes and approaches, like the 2024 Tanzanian conference co-organized by the African Peace and Education Association (AFPREA), the Association of Catholic Universities and Higher Institutes of Africa and Madagascar (ACUHIAM), the Pan-African Nonviolence and Peacebuilders Network (PANPEN), the Africa Peace and Development Network (MAMA), the MS Training Center for Development Cooperation (MS TCDC), and St. Augustine University of Tanzania (SAUT). The conference theme of "Ujamaa, Ubuntu, and New Pan Africanisms: The Future of World Peace" offered a Sankofa vision: looking at the past to build lessons for the future. In its call for papers, the coalition organizers noted that their plan was to create "a unique multi-location activity taking place in several venues throughout the East Africa country."

24 Archbishop Tutu kindly provided the introductions to the War Resisters League 1993 Peace Calendar, Children of War, Children of Peace: Youth and Resistance, as well as the biography of Oscar Lopez Rivera, *Between Torture and Resistance,* PM Press, 2013.

The Call Continued:

"Both an ideology of economic solidarity and a political program developed by Nyerere's administration, Ujamaa was an experiment in economic democracy and African unity. Later, African ontologies, epistemologies, and political programs like Ubuntu gave rise to anti-colonial struggles that liberated communities from various forms of oppression while also building society on positive values.

"Pan Africanism emerged as a political program of decolonization, evolved into an ideology, and eventually was sentimentalized. However, we are now witnessing a renaissance of Pan Africanisms, with new efforts by young Africans, diasporans, and others restoring the political goals and social values of Pan Africanism while also questioning its shortcomings and gaps in relation to 21st-century peace amidst the pressures of neoliberalism.

"Our 2024 conference asks both what Pan Africanisms can do for Africa (including her diaspora), as well as what Pan Africanism offers to the world, and the future of peace."

Growing out of a series of continent-wide gatherings, including a 2014 South African conference that Archbishop Tutu presided over and that gave birth to the Pan-African Nonviolence and Peacebuilders Network, as well as a 2022 South Sudan two-week series of interconnected conferences and meetings of similar content, the Tanzania proceedings were small but impactful. African peace studies as a field had clearly developed into a mature part of the global peace research academy, and grassroots community organizers were incorporated into leading parts of this academic-activist consortium. It didn't signal a mass movement of Pan African radicalism, but it does signal the opportunities ahead for influential African-led peacemaking.

This peace-making paradigm parallels existing conversations taking place in what has been self-described as the Occupied People's Forum (OPF)—a broad network of still-colonized popular resistance movements bringing together strategists from Western Sahara and Ambazonia, from West Papua, Palestine, Puerto Rico, Kashmir, Kurdistan/Rojava, and Tibet. The OPF, led by but not limited to those territories, made particular connections during the South Sudanese peace weeks, as both Saharawi and Ambazonia representatives were vocal participants. Shifting emphasis just a little to focus on Indigenous perspectives within all of these movements, the plan to hold a high-level, in-person meeting became central to OPF's work—with the idea that various Pacific-island locations, such as Vanuatu and Fiji, could be perfect spots for such a convening. In addition to their own Indigenous-led movements and governments, which also include staunch support for the West Papuan independence cause, these island nations have long been part of the Nuclear Free Pacific campaigns that successfully link antimilitarist and anticolonialist concerns. This Afro-Asian alliance not only evolves from deep-rooted Pan-African histories (Nkrumah himself was removed from state power while traveling to China and Vietnam building bi-directional solidarity), it envisions a world of decentered, delinked,[25] multipolarities.

25 Samir Amin, *Delinking: Towards a Polycentric World,* Zed Press, 1990.

These notions are more in keeping with contemporary ideals of a pluriversal world "where many worlds may fit" than the current crisis of competing imperialisms and are open to including feminist notions combining the personal and the political. Indeed, one of Archbishop Tutu's best friends later in life was His Holiness the 14th Dalai Lama, whose sense of humor and mischievousness paralleled that of the Anglican cleric. Those two, however, were more than just joyous and playful friends[26]; their spiritual and political paths fit well together as concepts such as "middle way" policies sought and seek to find common "win-win" ground among opposing and conflicting sides.[27]

The onus, as usual, is on those with the most power to understand the long-term benefits of a sustainable world. Pan-Africanism may be the best means for the salvation of a continent and the peace of a planet, but it certainly remains a threat to all those profiting from the continued cheap or free extraction of extraordinary mineral, chemical, natural, and labor resources from the wealthy motherland. Kwame Nkrumah's visionary writings, like much of the Pan African classics, understood these power dynamics with a critical precision. As he put it, in ways that should challenge all peace advocates today:

"The danger to world peace springs not from the action of those who seek to end neocolonialism but from the inaction of those who allow it to continue."[28]

---

26 The Dalai Lama, Desmond Tutu, and Douglas Adams, *The Book of Joy: Lasting Happiness in a Changing World,* Avery, 2016.
27 His Holiness the Dalai Lama, *The Middle Way: Faith Grounded in Reason,* Wisdom Publishers, 2009.
28 Kwame Nkrumah, *Neocolonialism: The Last Stage of Imperialism,* PanAf Press, 2009, p. 259.

Chapter 5

Militants Not Militarists: Cabral's Forgotten Legacy

No contemporary review of existing African literature on peace, violence, nonviolence, war, and the causes of war could be complete without a serious consideration of the revolutionary movements of national liberation that engaged in protracted armed struggle and people's war to bring about an end to colonialism and independence and freedom for the masses. Too many pages have been filled with stories celebrating short-lived victories or decrying what should be seen today as temporary defeats. The struggle continues, and does so in many tactical and practical forms.

Amilcar Cabral is likely the most quoted and celebrated figure of the 1960s-'70s era armed combatants, whose legacy is cited and recited, in search of wisdom for today's freedom fighters. This is a more righteous endeavor than many; Cabral's gifts of strategic thinking and writing were many. Some aspects of his legacy—the penchant for extreme honesty, transparency, and love for the common people—are well worth examining and emulating. Other aspects of his teachings, as this essay suggests, remain sadly hidden, even in the current discourse. This essay, featured in the fine latest edition of edited commentary about Cabral (Manji and Fletcher, 2024),[1] attempts to spotlight some of Cabral's more hidden insights.

In 21st-century Africa, in contrast to the great Chinua Achebe's 65-year-old titular heading that "things fall apart," the continent is on the verge of achieving unprecedented modern greatness as "things come together." This pronouncement,[2] by no less a figure that Harvard University's Robert Rotberg, esteemed founding director of the JFK School of Governance Program on Intrastate Conflict, Conflict Prevention, and Conflict Resolution, stands as summary to a growing number of scholars and activists from a wide diversity of ideological perspectives who appear to unite around a generally all-African optimism. Perhaps the most noted and quoted 20th-century African figure central to parts of this positive thinking is Amilcar Cabral, correctly understood as one of the great visionaries of the century. Is the iconization of Cabral, however, as good as it should be or are some still missing the point?

It is in many ways fitting that Amilcar Cabral should be inextricably linked to the quote that best showcases his faith in and love for the people as a whole. Cabral's "Tell no lies" truth-cry was of course more than simply a call for honesty and transparency in life, love, and revolutionary work, it was and is a call for serious reflection on how we build our organizations and cadre in relationship

---

1 Manji, F. and Fletcher, B. (eds.). *Claim No Easy Victories,* Ontario: Daraja Press, 2023.

2 Rotberg, R. *Things Come Together—Africans Achieving Greatness in the Twenty-First Century,* arranged by Robert Rotberg. Oxford: Oxford University Press, 2020.

to the people. The period between Cabral's assassination and the movements of today illustrate easily enough that we can't claim any easy victories; we can barely claim victories at all! What then, in Cabral's vision and practice, suggests what we should and can do.

Now no movement or leader should be judged by a single quote. That reductionist technique always robs readers of historical context, strategic thinking, and the tactical possibilities for future advancement. Thus, as inspiring as Rev. Dr. Martin Luther King, Jr.'s "having a dream" might be to many people, that quote does much injustice to both the man and the Black-led, Southern-based freedom movement (as Vincent Harding urged, we more correctly call the "civil rights" movement). King was, of course, so much more than a dreamer. And the five years he lived following that classic speech contained more radical, internationalist insights and sharpened statements, that to focus on MLK in the summer of 1963 as an almost freeze-framed icon robs him of a half-decade of his actual lived experiences.

The "Claim no easy victories" excerpts from Cabral's 1965 directive must therefore be seen at best as the tip of a rather monumental iceberg that contains wisdom for our current period well beyond that admonition. To put Cabral's directive in historical context, he must have been well aware of the independence movements that preceded him, notably the successful Indian movements of the 1940s, the West Africa movements of the 1950s, and the victorious Cuban revolution of 1959. Keeping in mind that Cabral's directive was explicitly to the guerilla fighters of the African Party for the Liberation of Guinea and Cape Verde (PAIGC), this context—from Gandhi's nonviolence to Che's foco-ism with Pan Africanist, Pan Americanist, and communist thinking included—the whole of the "Claim No Easy Victories" directive is most extraordinary.

Cabral's is clear that his approach and that of the PAIGC must be centered on building "confidence in the future" based on "the joy of living" and with "love for life and its amusements." The passionate, steadfast, persistent love we must have for the people is, in this case, not primarily a theoretical or metaphoric concept but one borne of practicality from modern revolutionary experience. Like Mohandas Gandhi of India, whose "satyagraha" is as much a testament to "love-force" as the more commonly but not more powerful interpretation of that phrase as "truth-force" or "soul-force," the idea that the power of love is a strategic and tactical weapon is not new. In that way, Gandhi inhabits a sometimes uncomfortable marriage with Che, who taught that all great revolutionaries are mainly guided by love. Che recognized that some among his cadre would find the notion ridiculous, but he risked making his proclamation loudly, even in the midst of open warfare and enemies from the right and left. Iconic Che-in-Beret, like Sainted Gandhi, together forecast that many of our most cherished 20th-century dichotomized notions about radical social change have little bearing on our current realities. Pacifists can no longer suggest a monopoly on "loving thy neighbor" (especially when some of them seem to find loving nonarmed bureaucratic upholders of the violent status quo much easier than loving armed radical combatants). Armed radicals must take great care not to equate their choice of weapons with some secret ability to win greater victories or build more successful revolutions; history has not borne out their bold assertions. It is in this context that Guinea-Bissau's Amilcar Cabral may serve as best man to the as-of-yet unconsummated union between Gandhi and Che.

Therefore, especially for those peace and antiwar organizers among us, the more forgotten phrase of that famous speech takes on great significance today. Both traditional revolutionary nationalist strategies (as differentiated from the "change the world without taking power" approach) and the inadequacies of standing armies to provide effective lasting defense of peoples come to the fore. Cabral, decades before many of these generations-old false dichotomies were fully played out, had the vision and brilliance to implore that being an exemplary militant meant opposing militarism in all its forms.

Long before Mozambicans began wondering whether the symbol of the AK-47 rifle on the flag—despite all that it meant in the war for independence—was the best long-term image for the building of a new nation with generations who would oppose violence, Cabral had the vision and precision of words that should now echo North and South regarding "What is to be done." There is no coincidence that Mozambique's former minister of defense and first lady Graca Machel became the worldwide spokesperson for the elimination of all child soldiers, but that peacekeeping initiative must be seen in the context of Cabral's teachings based on a love for the people that transcended momentary victories on a given, singular battlefield. The Gandhi-Che-Cabral-and-beyond love of the people resonates with a sense of practical power shifts that require ways of feeling, thinking, and working past our old and current silos.

Cabral as commander of the armed forces had little reason to be optimistic in 1965 about the prospects for victory. In close contact with revolutionaries in Mozambique and Angola, with armed combatants and military leaders in other parts of Africa as well as supporters, including Fidel Castro in Cuba and especially Marxists who understood the importance of the freedom struggles in Africa, Cabral understood the dynamics of the "savage war of peace" that the Algerian Forces of National Liberation had to wage to rid their country of French political control. Cabral was of the generation and ideological circle that believed that armed struggle would be a prerequisite to any successful revolution.

Yet unlike any of these contemporaries—in Africa or anywhere else on the planet—Cabral reached back as a way of looking far into the future, drawing on the South African ANC leader and chief Albert Luthuli and others, who were rooted in building radical nonviolent movements (though they did not stand in the way when armed units and organizations were formed). Cabral proclaimed to his armed forces the still-under-quoted and under-analyzed directive on militants vs. militarists. Somehow Cabral's vision was sharp enough to understand that the tendency toward militarism and an overreliance on the power of military strategy by itself "must be urgently fought and eliminated within the army."

Cabral's broad vision of revolutionary victory was tied closely to the unarmed civilian resistance discussed among some popular academics today. Rather than "discover" the power of civil society, these mainly northern, western, and Euro-American academics would do well to look more closely at the wisdom of the Pan Africanists among whom Cabral was singularly important. There can be little doubt that Cabral was influenced by Kenneth Kaunda, whose rise to the presidency of Zambia the year before Cabral's iconic speech, and by Tanzania's Julius Nyerere. Both of these men had studied and worked with the nonviolent leaders of Rev. A.J. Muste in the USA and Rev. Michael Scott of the UK, and had relied on their solidarity and friendship. Pan African "people's ambassador" Bill Sutherland was serving at this time as a hospitality bridge between the armed and nonviolent, new governmental, and national liberation movements debating strategies and tactics at this time. When Kaunda took the top seat in government in Lusaka, he convened a summit of Sutherland, Muste, Scott, and others, with talk of building a nonviolent training center akin to a "nonmilitary West Point." Kaunda challenged them, however, with questions they were unprepared for: "How," he asked, "will newly independent Zambia which I am now responsible for, defend itself from the highly armed Rhodesians and apartheid South Africans at or near our borders, undermining our every move and denying our sovereignty? How can we defend our borders, much less build a national and regional movement which will ensure peace and freedom for all Africans?" Decades later, as Kaunda and Sutherland had a reunion in which this author was present, it was clear that there was no good answer that anyone came up with.

Writing and speaking one year later, Amilcar Cabral's words take on special meaning. He was going to forge ahead to lead the revolutionary movements so needed across the continent and the world. But he was not going to repeat past mistakes or lose the nuances learned in the previous decade of struggle. He would build, or attempt to build, a new type of armed force and a new society in the wake of its victory. Thus his "NO LIES" phrase focuses not simply on the act of being honest and humble but on, in his own words, having militant cadres see as their primary work to "create schools and spread education," to "work daily for the improvement of...cultural formations." Decision-making, what Cabral called "revolutionary democracy," meant that leading cadres' work was not to build alternative political structures for the Guinea-Bissau or Cape Verdean populations but to "normalise the political life of the people—explain to the population what is happening in the struggle." If the armed liberation forces' work was chiefly to "reinforce the mobilisation and organisation of the populations," it would more easily be able to follow the main truth thunderously spotlighted in his 1965 directive: oppose tendencies to militarism.

Amilcar Cabral was a militant revolutionary who understood that one not only could but must also be an antimilitarist. More than most radicals at the time or since, Cabral bridged the gaps between previous radicals, asserting a politics that built upon notions of people's democracy that went far beyond the social democrats of the day. His legacies for peace movements, civil resistance, and social change tacticians are at least equal to the Africanist leadership legacies he is already appropriately accorded.

Chapter 6

Africa's New Mwalimus: Teaching the World Afro-Feminist Lessons

Could a smile be so bright and inviting, so filled with energy as well as the challenge to join in, can such a smile be described as revolutionary? Entering almost any room, the large figure of Mawina Sowa Kouyate—founding leader of the All-African Peoples' Revolutionary Party (AAPRP)—filled the space with questions, passion, information, and that smile. Mawina's somewhat enigmatic legacy can obscure the extraordinary influences that she had on almost everyone she encountered during her decades as a US-based organizer's organizer. Her reply whenever asked where she was from was a generic and politically factual "I am from Africa." Despite that being personally untrue from a purely geographical perspective, it was just as deeply concrete and essential as her assertive self-description as Kwame Ture's sister had no biological basis in family history. An all-encompassing humanitarian internationalist, Mawina's profound and eminently practical love for "the people" left no doubt that hers was a Pan-Africanism ever ready for the revolution.

One of the great privileges of my life—far beyond those of the gender or race I was born into—was meeting Mawina and being encouraged to adopt her as a mentor when I was still a late teenager, just starting my path as a political activist and thinker. The summer and fall of 1980 in New York City were whirlwind times, so many parts of the story of that period often get omitted in the flurry of news about a given national election or excruciating assassination. The whole world remembers that in December of 1980, John Lennon was killed in front of the building and city he called home, shattering the idealist dreams of an exuberant comeback filled with a fusion of the personal, political, and cultural genius of someone ever-willing to imagine new ways of building society. Some may recall that the previous July saw the Democratic National Convention, held in NYC's Madison Square Garden, where President Jimmy Carter easily won his party's nomination to run for a second term despite an unpopular first four years.

One aspect of the critiques against Carter that cut across class, race, and age lines was his insistence to bring back the first phase of the draft—the wartime policy so divisive during the Vietnam era that it was abolished five years earlier almost as soon as the conflict in Southeast Asia ended. The major NYC coalition working against this call for "draft registration" was part of the New York Mobilization for Survival (MFS), and Mawina had recently been hired as part of their core staff. At the very end of my seventeenth year, I was seriously considering becoming a federal felon by breaking the registration law in the most public ways possible; I was also an incoming freshman at New York University and stumbled into the MFS offices three blocks from where most of my classes were being held to find out more about what I could do to resist. What I learned from MFS, and especially from Mawina, opened up a world of realities well beyond anything a course at NYU could explain. Those lessons have lasted fresh in my mind and stuck with me more than any professor's lecture or advice.

Africa Is on the Move!

I still have the African-published edition of Sekou Toure's 1967 book, outlining his vision for the liberation of Guinea. This is before my first trip to the continent, which took place just following Samora Machel's signing of the controversial Nkomati Accords between Mozambique and South Africa, when I was part of a Quaker-led delegation that had a special relationship with the Organization of Mozambican Women (OMM). Mawina was proud of the depth of my commitment, eagerly taking every NYU course having anything to do with Africa (there weren't that many!), and adding to them courses by leading Latin American, Asian, and Middle Eastern professors.[1] But her approach, one worth noting decades later and filled with still-vital advice, was to look for the utility to the common person present or lacking in any study, travel, or work opportunity that might come up. Without that key element, the endeavor, however apparently admirable, would simply not be worth the effort.

Mawina was the strongest and most compelling of a number of key voices around MFS of that period—including feminist Grace Paley; Black Veteran organizers Mustafa Randolph and Job Mashiriki; Harlem Fightback founder Jim Haughton; SNCC

1 Appropriate thanks here is due to NYU Professors Richard Hull, Warren Dean, Marilyn Young, Ahmed Ashraff, and Bertel Ollman, all of whom bucked the trend of complacency, and supported my education both academically and as an activist. Vic and Barby Ulmer of Our Developing World and OMM Secretary General Salome Moiana are also worthy of special note.

Freedom Singers Matt Jones, Rev. Fred Kirkpatrick, and Cordel Reagon; MFS organizers Norma Becker, Vivian Stromberg, Nora Lumley, and others. It was an eclectic group that included opportunities for me to work directly as an assistant to 1960s icon Abbie Hoffman, compiling a mailing list for him from the letters he received while in prison. Following a speech in which I announced my refusal to be drafted, I sang on stage with Pete Seeger and throngs of others at a 10,000+ rally in front of the UN demanding that US intervention in Central America be immediately and unconditionally ended. But the words of Mawina, busy building the All-African Women's Revolutionary Union, had the most profound effect. Along with Grace Paley and the Black Veterans for Social Justice, the urging to me, for all the boys of my generation, was not to repeat the mistakes of my elder brothers. Unlike the 1960s draft resisters, they insisted that we not focus our resistance movements and work solely on ourselves, and the mainly middle- or upper-class and predominately white males who would take the risk of going public with our refusals to comply with the federal law. Black, Brown, and Indigenous peoples—people of African descent especially—had always borne the brunt of US imperialist wars. And women of all backgrounds had always led resistance movements, though they were often unrecognized, uncredited, and not in the leadership positions of most of the national and international peace groups of the time.

Another AAPRP leader moved to New York around the time that Mawina joined MFS staff. Bob Brown, one of the oldest and closest comrades of AAPRP founder Kwame Ture (aka Stokely Carmichael), joined MFS National staff as Mawina joined their New York office staff. Both explained patiently to the curious white peace movement activists surrounding them that, when asked, Kwame explained that the principled white folks within the US empire who were worth working with were those who, during the Vietnam antiwar era and the turning tides from his leadership in the Student Nonviolent Coordinating Committee to Black Power to the Black Panthers to the AAPRP, neither turned their back on him nor rejected these changes outright. Ture assessed that most of those peace veterans congregated around Dave Dellinger and other radical antimilitarists, those now working to coalesce around the Mobilization for Survival (MFS)—an outgrowth of the Mobilization Committee to End the War in Vietnam. MFS was hardly a long-term comfortable space for Mawina or Bob, but it provided an opportunity to help build what would become the largest peace mobilization in US history to date: the June 12, 1982, Disarmament March on the United Nations.

Bob was an old hand at mass mobilizations, having worked all those decades with the man he still had permission to call Stokely; he went on, after 1982, to continue in this work as logistics coordinator of the Washington, DC, Million Man March and many other huge coalition gatherings. He and Mawina also helped build, back in 1982, a "third way" coalition between the in-fighting peace groups looking to gain the upper hand in two competing coalitions. The impetus for the June 12 mobilization focused on the UN Special Session on Disarmament, which itself was based on a call from UN member-states from the Global South who had pressed the global body to work toward linking arms control and human needs, even though all of the superpowers were engaged in an escalation of weapons. Mawina and Bob, along with comrades from throughout the Global South as well as organizations within the USA who were not yet part of the competing peace coalitions, formed the Third World and Progressive People's Coalition, which went beyond the MFS and others. Led by African and US Black liberation forces, it linked with many others including the leaders of progressive nation-states working within the UN. I happily worked in solidarity with these efforts, as the US Student Association and Progressive Student Network, which I represented at the time, was a part of all the main coalition entities working to make June 12 the largest peace mobilization in US history up to that time.

Mawina also explained, when asked, that she was from "Africa," though some deeper digging would reveal that she had barely ever set foot on the continent, coming via the "African" section of Boston, Massachusetts. A revered grassroots housing rights advocate, she taught by example, and the lessons of being a powerful, self-assured woman were at the forefront of her strength and determination. Like Kwame and Bob, she was also stridently committed to the empowerment of youth and students, analyzing young people as the motor force behind most world revolutions. Being a precocious young student leader, despite my non-African heritage, earned me some points I would guess, but I like to think my ongoing dedication to Pan-Africanism helped keep me in good graces. It couldn't have hurt that I was also a vocal, public draft resister, like Bob and Kwame before me (who, as Stokley, coined the slogan "Hell No, We Won't Go!). When our NYC student group convened a citywide founding conference, Kwame came in from his never-ending speaking tour to deliver a rousing address. Also providing inspiring speeches were Dave Dellinger, Grace Paley, and—in a historic reunion toward the end of her life—the extraordinary Ella Baker, who hadn't been in the same room with Kwame for many a decade.

When the US bombed Libya some years later, Kwame Ture led several delegations to Tripoli in direct challenge to the State

Department travel ban. On the anniversary of the bombing, internationalists from all over would join the Libya association the World Mathaba (meaning center) to view the wreckage in Tripoli, which had, among other losses, caused the death of Gaddafi's infant daughter. I was honored to be one of only two "white Americans" on one of those delegations, joining so many radicals from the AAPRP, the Provisional Government of the Republic of New Afrika, the Nation of Islam, the American Indian Movement, and other related groups.

Years later still, when Kwame was dying of cancer and in New York City to receive specialized treatment, his commitment to youth empowerment continued to shine. By that time, I was a high school teacher and my work was more centered in my connections to Mzee Bill Sutherland. But Kwame was thirsty for connections to the future, and his oratory, analysis, and vision were undeterred by his physical weakness. Mawina and I set up for a group of a dozen leading students to visit Kwame in the home where he was staying, complete with video cameras and loads of questions about a life well lived. For hours, we exchanged stories, news, frustrations, and plans for building a better world based on Pan-African unity and liberation. Kwame passed, Mawina passed, all things must pass. But the seeds of a future blessed by the warm sun and people's power of African liberation were sown deeply and continue to bear fruit.

Africa Is Woman!

Like most leftist men who became leaders during the radical 1960s, in the midst of the emergence of second-wave feminism, Kwame Ture was a complicated figure regarding women and leadership. We understand that there are few, if any historical figures who are not complicated. It is only the revisionists and sectarians, some many years later and far from the center of the scene, who try to avoid nuance and complication by painting people with an all-good or all-bad brush. In the business of movement-building, of organizing for the people like Mawina (and Kwame, and Bob), this divisiveness is especially dangerous. Complications and contradictions from one generation must be signposts for improvements for the next generation. It was in that spirit that Mawina Sowa Kouyate taught me, and in that same spirit that I raise, review, and reflect upon the following contemporary voices in urgent need of greater attention.

Lola Olufemi, in her book *Feminism, Interrupted: Disrupting Power*, cries out to us that "Solidarity is a doing word!" For us, this must be at the center of a redefined solidarity, a fully action-oriented conception that transcends simple "helping hands" connections. Mozambique's Samora Machel used to talk about solidarity as "two fists joined together to strike a single blow," and indeed those national liberationists fighting against Portuguese colonialism made special alliances with their Portuguese radical counterparts, also keen to emphasize the systems of imperialism, capitalism, and colonialism as the enemy. Olufemi takes these principles a step further, noting that

> Solidarity has always been at the heart of feminist practice. Ideas of 'global sisterhood' rose to prominence in the late twentieth century...its advocates called for the need to view women's liberation across borders and continents. Although this relied on the flawed concept of a 'universal patriarchy,' it opened up space to consider the power of refusing to remain divided by something as arbitrary as geographic location.

> There is no local without a global. There is no better answer to combat a fractured society obsessed with individualism than a politics that connects the dots. When we show solidarity to one another, we are demonstrating that we recognize that politics happens everywhere, at every level, in every region of the world.[2]

Olufemi correctly concludes that solidarity, in an internationalist context, requires "an emergent political practice." She includes in this emergent praxis a need for flexibility, for solution-oriented, bottom-up thinking, and for a constant commitment to redistribution of wealth and resources. For peacemakers, these connections are indispensable in understanding why violence and war seem so permanent. Without the feminist, socialist, Africanist notions articulated by Olufemi, there can be no peace.

Contemporary feminists and Global South women's rights advocates also have written insightfully about the violence-nonviolence paradigm and the many confusions and false dichotomies still asserted in traditional male-dominant Western theory and practice. Elsa Dorlin, for example, in her *Self Defense: A Philosophy of Violence*, underscores the race-gender connections so fundamental to modern-day racialized violence and patriarchal war-mongering on the battlefields and in the home. "The drive to establish a bourgeois patriarchy, with its own police," Dorlin writes, "and to take up dominant gender norms (which are white by definition) as a regulating ideology represents one of the most effective and consistent modalities of an apparatus of

2 Olufemi, Lola. 2020. *Feminism, Interrupted: Disrupting Power*. London: Pluto Press.

domination."[3] She asserts, in what must be a vital consideration for all those working for positive social change anywhere, that these particularly effective forms of domination, those incorporating race-gender-class connections, strike at the most vulnerable parts of social movements and mobilizations. The obvious and important implication is that any form of people's power, from peace work to peace education, from self-defense training to the building of alternative institutions, will be at a "dead end" if it does not deal with these class, race, and antipatriarchal struggles.

Unlike Pan Africanist teachings, these critiques and improvements of the discourse on solidarity and self-defense are universalist and not African-centered per se. Though informed by African historiography and lived experience, the lessons spring from and are centered in more international norms. The work on *The Invention of Women* by Oyeronke Oyewumi, however, takes a decidedly African and Yoruba-based research perspective and extends it to the disciples of decolonized academic pursuits as a whole and a decolonized peace studies in particular. Through extensive data-collection on linguistics, cultural anthropology, history, and other fields, Oyewumi describes how "women" as a distinctive social category did not exist in precolonial Yoruba societies. This is not to say that women did not exist, simply that the materialist categorization of them as a potentially oppressed "other" was not part and parcel of the makeup of early Yoruba society. She explains:

> The assertion that "woman" as a social category did not exist in Yoruba communities should not be read as

3 Dorlin, Elsa. 2017. *Self Defense: A Philosophy of Violence*. London: Verso Press.

> anti-materialist hermeneutics, a kind of post structuralist deconstructing of the body into dissolution. Far from it—the body was (and still is) very corporeal in Yoruba communities. But, prior to the infusion of Western notions into Yoruba culture, the body was not the basis of social roles, inclusions, or exclusions. It was not the foundation of social thought and identity. Most academic studies on the Yoruba have, however, assumed that 'body-reasoning' was present in the Yoruba indigenous culture. They have assumed the Western constructions as universal, which has led to the uncritical usage of these body-based categories for interpreting Yoruba society historically and in the contemporary period.[4]

This information is essential if we are to be in the business of publishing new books on new thinking about peace, social justice, and organizing for change. It is fundamentally important if we are to hope to build movements (and academic centers for actual learning) that seek not to replicate the diseased and violent structures of the past, but rather to work for lasting peace. If, as Oyewumi describes, Yoruba continues to be "a genderless language in a genderful world," and if the Yoruba and other matriarchal practices are not to be treated as panaceas or utopias but rather as experiences to learn from, we had better get our thinking caps on. What does it mean to build spaces for thought, including progressive publishing houses and book series and professional associations, if the very notion of how and what it means to be a human is inherently

4 Oyewumi, Oyeronke. 1997. *The Invention of Women: Making an African Sense of Western Gender Discourses.* Minneapolis: University of Minnesota Press.

misunderstood? If "identity" becomes a wholly malleable and shifting notion, how can we examine history from a Sankofa, forward-to-the-future perspective?

This is not to say that we must fall back on rigid binaries. It is to suggest that decolonized academic and activist work must be rooted in more than Westernized and largely male-defined notions of gender ideology, more than Westernized notions of "acceptable, modernizing" imperialisms, more than Orwellian notions of war and peace, and much, much more than silo-ized notions of "expert" peacemaking techniques, nonviolent trainers, or official conflict resolution specialists! There is, quite literally, an ever-growing world of new teachers—modern Mwalimus—who need to be recognized, published, read, interrogated, and dialogued with. We must, again as Elise Boulding was urging, prepare to learn from and not just about our African sisters and brothers. We must, as Mawina Kouyate and Kwame Ture constantly commanded, be Ready for Revolution!

Chapter 7

The Passage of White Power

In a little-known introduction to a hard-to-find 1978 book on "Rhodesian Guerillas," James Baldwin delves into the heart of white supremacy and whiteness. He begins, as any honest analyst of social change in the late 20th century must, with the work of W.E.B. DuBois, who famously wrote that the problem of that century was one of "the color line." Baldwin asserts that only those who had to pay attention to that fact did so; those who imagined themselves white, with little understanding of the past or the present, could choose to ignore these prescient words by the father of modern sociology[1].

> "[Whites] believe," Baldwin wrote, that the past and the present "are in their custody, and at the dictates of their power: this is the most cruel and dangerous delusion of our age...
>
> "White people really appear to believe that they are the authors, and custodians, of civilization, and that they are

1 Baldwin, J. 1978. Introduction, in Raeburn, M. *We Are Everywhere: Narratives from Rhodesian Guerrillas.* New York: Random House.

to be revered, and above all loved, for having played so noble and indispensable a role...

"I should imagine that the white delusion has something to do with the brief and blatant passage of their power."

I wrote the book *White Lives Matter Most*[2] as a descriptor of the US prehistory and history that required a movement for Black lives to emerge as one possible antidote to US settler colonial white supremacy. At the time, even when we wrote openly about the end of the empire, the still-powerful nature of white supremacy was also evident. This, however, was still well before the Trump-era rise of various right-wing and neofascist formations in the US that have served to strengthen divisions among people along a wide range of lines. That white supremacy in the US now coexists with a growing block of anti-immigrant Lantinos and a few self-proclaimed "Black Nazis" does not weaken Baldwin's analysis or the contemporary struggle to do away with delusions of grandeur and white power narratives.

It is noteworthy that some of these conversations come in the context of looking at and learning from Africa. Baldwin had no particular connection to the southern African liberation movements, but was perfect to write the introduction, in part because the book's author was a white Rhodesian sympathetic to the guerilla independence movement and because Baldwin had a profound understanding of the dynamics of otherness from all sides of the oppressed/oppressor divide. He understood what some now think of as an "Ubuntu" context, that one's humanity

2 Meyer, M. 2018. *White Lives Matter Most and Other "Little" White Lies.* Oakland: PM Press.

is fully wrapped up in and only fully realized in connection to the "other." For 1978, as for 2025 as well, Baldwin understood that "we are beginning to live through the beginning of the end of the nightmare of color, and if this is freedom for the black man (sic), it will bring to the white man (sic) a joy and a freedom he does not, now, dare imagine."

I have long asserted that the great privilege I've enjoyed as an adult has not been my birth into a place and time where I was considered both white and male without question. It was clear that at least one of those assumptions would not have been true had I been born a mere fifty years earlier and several thousand miles further to the east. The privileges I've most enjoyed have all centered on living out the daily realities of making peace and solidarity with African peoples from all walks of life, of exquisite travel and profound education, of love and liberation, and, ultimately, of building a family that literally transcends racial, ethnic, cultural, and other "norms." The ability to imagine and enact a disempowered whiteness, to find power in the successes and liberation of others, suggests not only giving up certain privileges and powers but also remaining open to critique, reconsideration, and ongoing acts of reparation. It means never resting on one's laurels or one's privileges.

The first conversation between Africa World Press founder Kassahun Checole and I regarding an Africa World Peace book series involved an honest assessment of whiteness and leadership in an influential editorial position. Beyond the niceties of my own deserving *curriculum vitae* and lifelong Pan African experiences, beyond the fact that the two of us would be working together closely and surrounded by a majority-Africa Board of Advisors and coeditors, beyond even that the world at this moment was ready to begin what Jimmy Baldwin suggested was beginning over forty years ago, there was something else. We deeply believe that beyond institutional academic excellence, we can only be true to the goals of such a series by working to engage and involve truly international movements of people, that is, grassroots people from every sector, continent, and sociocultural identity group that humanity has to offer. An unconscious or semiconscious relationship to race and ethnicity, a nontransparent structure with "race neutral" or negligent pretenses that "those things don't matter so much any more" will signal an early defeat for what we are trying to do. We are not at the end of the end of Baldwin's and all of our nightmares, and if we are at a middle stage since he wrote those words, as we are at a maturing stage in the field of African Peace Studies, we had better be prepared to look at our issues of privilege, power, race, class, and gender, directly and forthrightly. We had better be able to look one another in the eye: directly, deeply, and respectfully.

In that context, the words of young US-based writer, singer, mother, and self-described Ubuntu Freedom organizer, YahNe Ndgo, have updated Baldwin in a manner he surely would have appreciated. A member of the Black Alliance for Peace and part of a new generation of activist/cultural workers who provide staunch support for today's political prisoners (including the elders), Ndgo has asserted:

> Some of my favorite people are white. And yes, I know how that sounds. But I don't say that to prove I'm not prejudiced. I say that to contextualize my prejudice. When it comes to the struggle for Black liberation, and my perspective on the liberation of our Brown brothers and sisters, I am prejudiced against white participation.

> This is antithetical to who I am, which makes it a struggle. It's a struggle because I believe in our fully equally connected humanity. It's a struggle because I know that white people need to be liberated too. But the reality is that very few white people can stop being white, and whiteness is violence. Whiteness is full-on colonization in every part of the world in which it has any traction but some of Europe. Colonization is the erasure of the culture, the insights, the magic, the humanity, and the bodies of everyone else, everyone who preceded the colonizer. That is violence.[3]

Anyone of any ethnicity, race, or nationality professing to be a modern-day peacemaker who doesn't understand the profound, 21st-century decolonizing truths articulated by Ndgo will hit a roadblock on the path to liberatory movement-building. They won't get stuck because they have bad intentions, and not because they are inherently bad people. They won't get stuck because of their identity within the human family or even because of their lack of experience as social change workers. They'll get stuck—and we are collectively stuck in too many corners of our beloved planet—because we are hiding from these fundamental historical truths. When Sister dequi kioni-sadiki and I, along with Baba Sekou Odinga of the New York Black Panthers and cofounder of the Panther International Chapter, set out to put out *Look for Me in the Whirlwind: From the Panther 21 to 21st-Century Revolutions* (PM Press, 2017), we were

3 YahNe Ndgo, "Made with Real Sugar" from YahNe Ndgo I Am Because You Are: The Writings website page, https://www.yahnendgo.com/made-with-real-sugar/, Accessed 24 November 2024.

sure to begin with the words of classic historian John Henrik Clarke. He noted that "history is a compass," one that "people use to find themselves on the map of human geography....It tells them where they are but, more importantly, what they must be."[4] The old African proverb has much wisdom: "Until the lions have their own historians, the stories will always make the hunter the hero." But Baldwin is also correct: somehow white folks, even well-intentioned ones dedicated to revolution, center them/ourselves in the histories we tell. The white supremacist socialization we all have been through teaches us well the "rationality" of it all.

YahNe Ndgo is correct: Whiteness is nothing but violence. That obviously doesn't mean that everything every white person does is violent; John Brown, Marilyn Buck, Ruth Reynolds, and many others have taught us that. But it does mean that any white "nonviolent activist" who doesn't take these realities and histories into account cannot help but perpetuate more violence than they even understand. (White folks who thoughtlessly or ahistorically advocate armed struggle as a knee-jerk tactical reaction to any situation do the same!). Ndgo is correct, and the only path to full-on decolonization must be paved with a consciousness of these global socializations. That is why some of those coming out of the radical movements of past generations formed white-only solidarity groups that worked under the direct leadership of national liberation movements. They didn't have all the answers either, but as folks who had a consciousness around many of these issues, they are too often dismissed as somehow naïve or out of step when in

4 Kioni-sadiki, d. and Meyer, M. (editors), Look for Me in the Whirlwind: From the Panther 21 to 21st Century Revolutions, PM Press, 2017.

fact they were trying to participate in the broader struggles while also taking their whiteness out of the organizational equation as much as possible. To dismiss these attempts as foolish is White Supremacy talking.

Ndgo is correct, and that is why any Peace Studies, especially African and Global South-centered Peace Studies, must confront the passage of White Power.

Chapter 8

A New Day for Pan-African Peace Studies: Arusha and Mwanza, Tanzania 2024

This report and the following short anecdote are versions of articles and dialogues appearing in the newsletters and meetings of the International Peace Research Association and the Africa Peace Research and Education Association (AFPREA). One of the original documents included assistance and coauthorship from Kenyan AFPREA leader Jacinta Mwende. They appear here in excerpted form, both to bring up to date the history of the field of African Peace Studies, as well as to spotlight some contemporary thorns in dealing with racism and assumptions within our movements.

From 23 to 27 May 2024, a series of meetings held in northern Tanzania set forth a vision of a new Pan-Africanism fully relevant for the current century, based on academic and data-driven contemporary research as well as activist wisdoms gleaned from ancient Indigenous to very modern times. This all could describe the biennial conference of the Africa Peace Research and

Education Association (AFPREA), which did serve as the initiator of and container for these meetings, but the gatherings as a whole represented much more than that. Like the preceding AFPREA conference, held in South Sudan in 2022, the occasion of the biennial conferences of Africa's leading scholarly peace organization brought together interested parties from across the continent as well as across the fields of peace, human rights, decolonizing, and justice movements. In Tanzania, our collaboration bore greater fruits than ever, as we deepened our analysis of the period we face and the period just ahead.

First, it must be noted that the choices of Tanzania and Arusha were never random; the conference theme of "Ujamaa, Ubuntu, and New Pan-Africanisms: The Future of World Peace" was rooted in the rich history of Mwalimu Julius Nyerere's and the early African independence movement's hopes and dreams for an African-centered prosperity. The 2024 conference attracted many close collaborators and cosponsors, including the African Peacebuilding Network and New Generation scholars of the Social Science Research Council (SSRC); the Universal African Alliance Community Center (UAACC); the Mwamko, Solidarity Uganda (SU) and New Pan African/Africa Rising networks; the Association of Catholic Universities and Higher Institutes of Africa and Madagascar (ACUHIAM); the Pan African Nonviolence and Peacebuilders Network (PANPEN); the webinar-based Africa Peace and Development Network (MAMA); the Oppressed People's Forum (OPF); and the International Peace Research Association (IPRA). Hosted locally by the MS Training Center for Development Cooperation (MS TCDC) and St. Augustine University of Tanzania (SAUT), the gathering was largely self-funded from the bottom up, the coalition organizing did receive some funding from the SSRC, SU, IPRA, The Community Movement Builders, the AJ Muste Foundation, the Resistance Studies Initiative, and the Fellowship of Reconciliation (both US and Swedish). These names and titles, however impressive, do not tell the tale!

Well beyond the impressive list of collaborating organizations and individuals throughout the continent was the diverse nature of the participants. A truly multigenerational endeavor, the conference opened with true elders of the Tanzanian and Pan-African movements—those who worked most closely with Mwalimu Nyerere and the efforts for Ujamma and a new African vision. Nyerere's own right-hand man, former regional commissioner Joseph Butiku, started us off with stories of the past as well as information about the Nyerere Foundation that he now heads up. Next was eminent scholar and activist Issa Shivji, professor emeritus of public law and First Julius Nyerere Professor of Pan-African Studies at the University of Dar es Salaam. Shivji challenged us to look beyond simply "humanitarianism" to build a truly justice-based political economy that would serve all of humanity. Joining us virtually was former Tanzanian minister of lands, housing, and human settlements development Anna Kajumulo Tibaijuka, whose more recent work as the executive eirector of the United Nations Human Settlement Programme (and former UN under-secretary-general) has brought African wisdom and practice to global level of advancement. On the other end of the age spectrum, grassroots activists Alieu Bah of the Gambia and Kenya's Sungu Oyoo, both with the Mwanko network, served as facilitators for much of the conference opening infusing a youthful revolutionary activist spirit to our intellectual and academic content. In between the youth and elders, those who have become "regulars" in the building of these gatherings—AFPREA's Charles Wasike, PANPEN's Moses Monday and Light Aganwa, the Catholic Universities' network George Mutalemwa, Pax Christi International's Sister Teresia Wamuyu Wachira, and your two authors (Jacinta representing the SSRC African Peacebuilders and Matt representing IPRA)—were present throughout to help bridge old and new thinking, as well as activist and academic approaches.

The Arusha conference also built strongly on the commitments made two years prior at the AFPREA conference held in Juba, South Sudan. For many in attendance at that 2022 summit, it seemed obvious to declare a "Juba moment": the ushering in of a more mature, unified, nuanced, and developed field of African and Pan-African Peace Studies. Now, standing even more as Africans and Pan-Africanists on our own, the global associations International Peace Bureau and the International Fellowship of Reconciliation were not significant cosponsors as they were in Juba, but the focus on still-colonized peoples set forth in Juba carried on to our 2024 meetings. Like Juba, a leader of the Western Sahara NOVA (nonviolent youth organization) was in attendance, as was author/educator Rudolf Nsang of Ambazonia (Cameroon), who updated us on the dire situation of the English-speaking population who are effectively under military occupation by the French neocolonial Cameroon armed forces. The Occupied People's Forum, which brought many together in Juba, was present through these representatives, joined by Colombia's Marcela Agudela-Ortiz and the USA's Jihad Abdulmumit—who helped extend the dialogue on principled decolonizing and antigenocidal struggle from Africa to Palestine to the entire world.

Abdulmumit, a major figure in the US's Black liberation movement and Muslim community, was also a significant part of another Arusha strengthening. Having presented the case for US human rights abuses and genocidal practices against its own Black, Brown, and Indigenous population at the Juba conference, Jihad further delineated the work of the Spirit of Mandela coalition and the efforts to build a voice and space for those disenfranchised within the US, a true Peoples' Senate that would be able to stand up to the US government's failing "two-party" imperial predicament. Unlike Juba, however, in Arusha, Abdulmumit was joined by an influential contingent of organizers from the US Black liberation movement, including the cofounders of what is often considered the most powerful grassroots initiative in the US South, Cooperation Jackson (and its leaders Kali Akuno and Saki Hall), the main Stop-Cop-City antipolice violence network Community Movement Builders (and its cofounder Edget Betru), as well as NYC Peoples' Senate activist Shannon Wills and Professor Latif Tarik, presenting on the ongoing relevance of Walter Rodney.

Taken as a whole, this was one of the most significant in-person exchanges between African and African Diasporic peoples this century, with a plan to continue to build these connections. At the center of these cross-continental conversations were the beautiful people of the UAACC—of Tanzanian and US birth, but forged together over the past three decades in an intensively grassroots Arusha-land-based community. UAACC's founders were refugees of the US government's admittedly illegal and murderous "Counterintelligence Program (COINTELPRO)" against Rev. Dr. Martin Luther King, Jr., Minister Malcolm X, the Black Panthers, and others; Pete and Charlotte O'Neal found a home in Tanzania in the 1970s, after fleeing the terror back home, and soon began building what would become the UAACC. In 2024, the AFRPREA conference official concluded at their annual African

Liberation Day (ALD) celebrations, held in a semi-developed rural space and filled with food, music, dance, artwork, poetry, a fashion show, singing, and a joyous review of what had come before and what we still must do to bear fruit.

ALD, however, was not the end of our 2024 work in Tanzania, despite the formal conference closing. Tanzanian co-coordinator George Mutalemwa, a professor at Mwanza's St. Augustine University of Tanzania (SAUT) and director of both ACUHIAM and Project MAMA, had long proposed the idea that this be a fully mobile conference, using the land and people of Tanzania itself as both "venue" and "workshop space" for the 2024 proceedings. Though the grand scope of moving an entire group of international conference attendees from one town to another to a third, stopping along the way to hold meetings and learn from the local people in each area, proved too logistically and financially complicated to achieve (this year!) on a large scale, a small group of participants (from North and South America, East and North Africa) did travel for several days to fulfil this expansive dream. Meetings were held with the Maasai peoples resisting corporate and governmental land grabs and climate crisis denialism, with Nyerere's own son Godfrey (himself an environmental activist and leader of the Nyerere Foundation), and with Catholic and other students and professors at SAUT and the city of Mwanza. SAUT Vice-Chancellor Ambassador Professor Costa Ricky Mahalu graced us with his presence as a closing afternoon of workshops were held virtually with speakers from around the world.

Perhaps MS-TCDC's academic dean Dr. Irene Lugalla said it best: "We have come together based on our shared histories, and together today we will make new history."

As MS-TCDC social movements and organizing expert Phil Wilmont movingly read a poem based on his experience taking seedlings from the gravesite of freedom fighter John Garang during the 2022 South Sudan conference, as we gathered around the small tree on the TCDC. Tanzanian campus where those seeds have taken root, we could feel the powerful presence connecting theory and practice; past, present, and future; our identities, conditions, and geographies. It was clear that we all still must build. It was truly historic to be part of these 2024 gatherings where such progress in a positive direction was made.

Chapter 9

US Privileges and Power at a Pan-African Conference

We stood at the cross sections between gender, race, class, age, and nationality. We were surely not friends but also not inclined to be enemies; we were unlikely to become comrades. We were on African soil, both connected but neither directly. She, a young US citizen of African descent, a successful academic with pride and poise, connected through intellectual prowess and historic genocide and oppression. Me, an old US citizen of European descent, bridging radical academic and activist pursuits, connected through a literal lifetime of personal and political actions taken since I was nineteen years old. From my Pan-Africanist step-dad of recognizable reputation, to the dozens of meetings, conferences, and events in every corner of the continent that I have attended, spoken at, co-organized, and helped raise funds for, my connections were well known and, in scholarly vernacular, eminently citable.

Our conflict burst through the otherwise friendly conversations. It was late in the evening of the last day of the international conference, at the café/bar area of the venue we were meeting in and staying at.

I was clear enough: In just a few hours before the break of dawn, a group of seven (the two of us included) were to depart for a two-day excursion that included enough unknowns to make anyone uncomfortable. The back story is relevant, but for now it is worth just writing that I was tasked by my African colleagues with the unenviable job of collecting money for the trip—and thus in some ways appeared as the organizer of this excursion. The company manager was up late and waiting to be paid. As we arrived at the café, I had still to collect money from some of the seven. Though all had confirmed and reconfirmed their participation and payment rate, I was over-tired and looking to make simple collections.

The first person I spoke with, not from the US, shared concerns about costs and return-trip logistics; we agreed to a subsidized rate that I was willing to help cover. The second, the elder good friend of my would-be nemesis, said that there were issues, that she had to make a phone call, and that she'd let me know soon what the deal would be. I was in shock. If she and her bestie were to pull out, almost half the cost of the trip could suddenly fall on me—an amount I could neither afford nor could my organization ever hope to recoup. I was shaken, angry, and scared...and I made no effort to hide or disguise this. The elder told me that she'd be good for her share and not to worry. But I was worried. And I somehow couldn't bring myself to trust her words.

I thought that I was quite clear, and this was the last possible, horrible moment. I went to the younger of the pair, sitting elsewhere with others—friends and comrades of us both. I wanted to simply ascertain if, as I suspected, she also was canceling her confirmed plans. And I needed to know about the money!

I was clear in my mind the basic elements: a number of African colleagues had worked hard on setting up this special experience,

I was made responsible for a portion of it, which seemed to be going south, and despite my occasional ability to pull fiscal rabbits out of empty hats, I was in this instance in a financially desperate situation, barely able to cover my own ticket.

My "clarity" was also absolutely wrong.

Without going into too many more of the specifics, my affect—my intensity, interruptive-ness, focus on money, lack of trust of the elder that she would "take care of it"—became elements of my identity, which also always include race, gender, and class. A more mature me should've not only been calmer (and yes, it was very late and I/we had worked very hard); I could well have been more trusting and patient despite the pressures. I most certainly also should not have taken on the "set-up" of the task in the first place. I was neither the best person nor the main person involved in the logistics of a region of a country where others had much more familiarity.

Something else occurred to several of us, as we processed the tensions with the help of our comrades. All of who I am and have been gave me a not-inappropriate feeling of comfort in this space, among the African comrades, and with friends and extended family members throughout the conference attendees. One of the keynote speakers, an elder and beloved Pan Africanist, had apparently cited, quoted from, and praised my book *Guns and Gandhi in Africa* for decades...a fact he made public in the course of his keynote speech! The comfort/discomfort level, however, especially in the context of our US citizenship and the racialized, engendered, and class conditions within the USA and its social change movements at this time, inherently made my "adversary" uncomfortable, in more ways than I could (or did) imagine. This wide gap of disconnection existed before either of us could even be fully aware of one another's presence or who we were as individuals in that space.

There were surely some things I should have done differently in the heated moment. But there may have been very little I could have done in general to remove these differences and divides between us regarding comfort and discomfort in the space of the conference—perhaps her first conference of this type in the motherland.

This is not to say that one can only shrug one's shoulders and say, "Oh well."

This is a small cautionary tale of the pernicious nature of power and privilege, and the need (especially for white cis males of the Global North) to remain ever vigilant. There are many good and great people all around us, and some good organizations and institutions as well. Good intentions certainly are not "good enough" as far as building future movements. This is because there are as many traumas, dysfunctions, diseases, and systemic evils similarly surrounding us, ready to lash out when we are most tired, frustrated, or yearning for a quick fix to a timeless problem. It is at these points that we must be most reflective—as a means of being strategic—about the whole of our interconnected and differing humanities. It is only with this heightened consciousness and action that we can use our powers with the appropriate imagination to produce (publish) effective works and build stronger movements for a better world.

Chapter 10

Our Words, Our Work, Our Movements

This is a time of redefinition. As several have noted over the past several years, redefining our terms of condition and practice is essential for facing the future. From a renewed commitment to decolonizing the academy, to a sharper analysis of the position of the nation-state as the motor force for revolutionary social change, we must devote our studies and our struggles toward imagining 21st-century social change constructs that learn true lessons from the liberation movements, constructive programs, daily acts of resistance, human-rights-based attempts at truth and reconciliation, and coalition united fronts that bring together ever-growing communities of people into strategic radical dialogue for collective work.[1] From the false dichotomies of Kingian nonviolence vs. Malcolmite "by any means necessary" approaches—like the false dichotomies clearly revealed by examination of the work of Albert Luthuli and the African National Congress Youth League—

1 These concepts of redefinition are treated in more detail in Meyer, M. 2022. "Decolonizing Peace Studies: Empowering Civil Society, Resisting the Causes of War." *Chinese Journal of Peace Studies*. Nanjing: Chinese Journal/Nanjing University.

we must continue to move past our grandfathers' battles and divisions to confront our own contradictions.

It is not surprising, then, that a number of places where our work has connected with redefining concepts and rewording our world have been within the field of peace studies, especially emanating from the Global South. Former IPRA secretary general Ursula Oswald Spring, professor at the National University of Mexico and former minister of environmental development in that country, coined the term "patriacene" to better describe the all-encompassing role of patriarchy as context for analyzing the past in search of new tomorrows.[2] The 2025 IPRA General Biennial Conference, the first global peace conference to be completely held on Indigenous land hosted by native people, was led by Māori scholar Kelli Te Maihāroa, author of leading texts on decolonizing peace and conflict studies through Indigenous research and "Indigenous autoethnography."[3] During and following the worldwide COVID-19 pandemic, a group of leading Latin American peace researchers detailed a wide-ranging constructive

---

2 The entire 50th anniversary issue of the foundational professional journal *Peace & Change* was devoted to new terms and new thinking in the field of peace studies. See *Peace & Change*. 2025. Volume 50, Number 1. London: Wiley/Blackwell. Specifically, note: Oswald Spring, U. 2025. Engendered-sustainable Peace in the Patriacene: Future threatened by violence, climate change, pandemics, and tipping points. *Peace & Change*. 2025. Volume 50, Number 1. London: Wiley/Blackwell. See also: Meyer, M. 2025. New Terms for a New Peace Studies: Introduction to the 2025 *Peace & Change* Special IPRA Issue, the 50th Volume of P&C. *Peace & Change*. 2025. Volume 50, Number 1. London: Wiley/Blackwell.

3 Te Maihāroa, K., Ligaliga, M., and Devere, H. (eds.). 2022. *Decolonising Peace and Conflict Studies through Indigenous Research*. London: Palgrave/Macmillan. See also: Te Maihāroa, K. and Adrian Woodhouse. 2024. *Indigenous Autoethnography: Illuminating Māori Voices*. London: Palgrave/Macmillan.

program campaign calling for a redefinition of our basic assumptions regarding what "normal" society should look like. Their text, *A New Normalcy,* has guided rethinking in that region regarding all levels of socio-political-economic sustainable development.[4]

In Africa, re-collecting and revising old practices to fit modern materialist realities have been a part and parcel of our various recent convenings. The 2024 AFPREA conference in Tanzania was not so much on the themes connecting Ujamaa and Ubuntu, but rather on re-appropriating and rethinking those concepts in their deepest 21st-century forms. For scholars of Nyerere and Tanzania's socialist experiments,[5] it will serve as little surprise that our revisions revealed what Nyerere noted toward the end of his life: It is not so much that the Ujamaa experiments failed, but rather that they were barely even attempted in the first place![6] Nyerere's friend and young scholarly protégé Issa Shivji delivered the keynote address at that 2024 conference, explaining his perspectives on the past and future of Ujamma:

> Many Western writers writing on Nyerere's concept of equality have totally missed the philosophical profoundness of Nyerere's concept. They have tended to assimilate it in the notion of Western concept of equality. Nyerere's

4 Ramos Muslera, E., Agudelo-Ortiz, D.M., and Kuhlmann, P. 2022. *Una Nueva Normalidad: Es Posible y Necesaria*. Tegucigalpa: Universidad Nacional Autónoma de Honduras/CLAIP.

5 See, for example, Shivji, I. 2008. *Pan-Africanism or Pragmatism. Lessons of the Tanganyika-Zanzibar Union.* Dar es Salaam: Mkuki na Nyota Publishers. See also: Maghanga, L. and Mwangi, N. (eds.). 2023. Ontario: Daraja Press.

6 Sutherland, B., and Meyer, M. 2000. *Guns and Gandhi in Africa: Pan African Insights on Armed Struggle, Nonviolence, and Liberation.* Trenton: Africa World Press.

> concept of equality based on human dignity imports as its integral part the notion of equity. Anything that offends human dignity is inequitable (see Shivji 2014). Poverty and disease offend human dignity; so do oppression, exploitation, unfreedom and torture. Needless to say, colonialism and imperialism are gross violations of human dignity. Thus, Nyerere had no problem in arriving at his conception of socialism from his philosophical premises. He once remarked that, "No one who qualifies his belief in the equality of man is really a socialist." (Nyerere 1968, pp.4-5)[7]

Shivji went on to assert that the very concept of individual "equal rights" as currently applied is unjust and inequitable. So long as capitalist, imperialist heteropatriarchy divides people along basic race/class/gender lines, there can be no equal rights per se. Reimaging Pan-Africanism, then, according to Shivji, requires a keen adversity to the status quo in this era of rampant imperialism and a voracious capitalist world order. Shivji suggests basic paradigm shifts required if a Pan African peace and justice are to prevail. These include redefining our work from a geographic vantage point to a social one, from one focusing on the unity of states to one centered on solidarity among peoples, and from human rights to human dignity. This latter point means moving away from "humanitarianism" (commonly understood as a charitable way of thinking) and toward an old/new idea about our interconnected "humanness" (rooted in solidarity among peoples). While echoing

7 Shivji, I. 2024. "Ujamaa, Ubuntu, and Reimagining Pan Africanism." Keynote Address at the International Conference on Ujamaa, Ubuntu and New Pan Africanisms, Arusha 23-25, May 2024. Dar es Salaam: Issa Shivji Papers.

critiques we have reviewed elsewhere, Shivji reaffirms and encapsulates in summary form the current prerequisites for successful revolutionary action.

It should be noted that there is no contradiction between this reassertion and deepening of socialist ideological development and the anti-authoritarian critical reviews of "politics at a distance from the state." The African and radical examples studied in the recent book of the same name begin from the perspective, now widely popularized by John Holloway, that nation-states inherently dilute, diminish, and ultimately kill off hope, by sending mobilized masses of people "home." Instead of intensifying, rearranging, and escalating the ever-needed tenets of evolving social change and permanent revolution, states suggest and assert that they (the elected officials, the self-proclaimed leadership circle, the dictatorships) will take care of things for We, the People. Simply put, the state is far from the best form of political organization for the ongoing project of popular liberation.[8] In thinking outside of the boxes that states have contained many of us in, research on questions of labor and land can bring us to new conceptions of the nature of democracy and citizenship.[9]

Still, the reason for suggesting that these ideas are "old/new" goes beyond an homage to Indigenous thought. A few visionary figures, Nyerere and Cabral among them, were clear a half-century ago of the trappings of what was being termed as revolution in the

8 Helliker, K., and Van der Walt, L. (eds.). 2018. *Politics at a Distance from the State: Radical and African Examples.* Oakland: PM Press.

9 Naicker, C., and Bruchhausen, S. 2018. "Broadening conceptions of democracy and citizenship: the subaltern histories of rural resistance in Mpondoland and Marikana." In *Politics at a Distance from the State: Radical and African Examples.* Oakland: PM Press.

heady 1960s. One good thing about the current resurgence of interest in Cabral among leftists in the Global North as well as Africa is the emphasis on his "emancipatory thoughts" about culture and his bottom-up trust and reliance on everyday people.[10] The small radical publishers behind 1804 Books saw fit to recently publish an English edition of Mario de Andrade's fine text, ***Amilcar Cabral: A Political Life in Motion***. In it, Cabral contemporary and dear Angolan friend, reviewing their work together studying the Vietnamese communist movements, resistance to colonialism, and independence movements, suggest that Cabral understood a "sociology of people's war"[11] that makes his contributions uniquely relevant. Known in his time as "the Engineer," Cabral was famous for living his life with the people, always open and anxious to learn from the common woman and man. His fusion of study and action led to some of the most revolutionary and postindependence examples of critical schooling, networks of preventative community-based health centers, and experiments with the commercialization of exports that centered peasants as the labor force most deserving to be compensated.

The debates about ideological rebuilding, redefinition of terms, and especially challenges to "new left" conceptions of the role of national liberation armed struggle as the vanguard forefront of revolutionary tactics are nowhere more intense than in Latin America. Holloway's impact on the Zapatistas, like their impact on him, is well documented. The work of other activist-scholars may be less spotlighted but are no less important. At a recent New York

10 Neocosmos, N. (ed.). 2021. *Politics and Culture in African Emancipatory Thought: Amical Cabral and Ernest Wamba-dia-Wamba*. Ontario: Daraja Press.
11 De Andrade, M. 2024 (English edition); 2014. *Amilcar Cabral: A Political Life in Motion*. New York: 1804 Books.

book launch of Uruguayan radical Raul Zibechi's ***Constructing Worlds Otherwise: Societies in Movement and Anticolonial Paths in Latin America***,[12] we discussed his experiences in building effective contemporary movements of struggle.

Today, more than ever, Zibechi noted, "place informs politics." We can no longer afford to attempt the development of new theory from a grand ideology, but rather must develop theory from practice and a practice where "we all are subjects." Though the repression and concerns about state power that have spread across the world have led to decentralized experiments, many of which are good, the nature of localized autonomous movements in and of themselves is challenging isolation. "Autonomy today is an island," Zibechi continued, with "many examples of little islands and little movements that we can build." We still need control of land and territory, however, because "when we don't have territory, we can speak about autonomy, but we cannot build it." Zibechi's sense of hope, however, is common among many of his peers: "In Latin America, our movements are creating a different world."[13]

These words echo the work, even government-based, of Vivian Camacho. The push for greater lasting progressive change often operates on an assessment that the two most important worldwide movements today are feminist and Indigenous movements. Zibechi calls the Global South women's movements "the vanguard of the resistance," in large part because they have trained themselves in creating collaborative organizations, while men continue more competitive forms of left institutional development.

12 Zibechi, R. 2024. *Constructing Worlds Otherwise: Societies in Movement and Anticolonial Paths in Latin America.* Chico: AK Press.

13 From a conversation with Raul Zibechi at the Woodbine Collective, New York, 20 April 2024.

Women-centered and Indigenous movements, for some, hold the hope of moving radical politics "beyond the impasse" of contemporary left malaise.[14] Another old/new notion centers feminist/women's movements, again especially of the Global South, with developing the spaces for more spiritual movements,[15] for more successful radical economic challenges,[16] and for developing the joyous positive components[17] of sustainable social change. Hope, joy, and a positive outlook are surely not the makeup of a sober, scientific approach. But they remain fundamental requirements of any attempt to make change.

---

14 Hardt, M., and Mexxadra, S. 2023. *Bolivia Beyond the Impasse*. Philadelphia: Common Notions.

15 Fernandes, Leela. 2003. *Transforming Feminist Practice: Non-violence, Social Justice and the Possibilities of a Spiritualized Feminism.* San Francisco: Arte Lute Books.

16 Disney. J.L. 2008. *Women's Activism and Feminist Agency in Mozambique and Nicaragua.* Philadelphia: Temple University Press.

17 Among many current writers taking this approach is the "applied utopia" work of the Slow Factory, including recent work by a founder, Semaan, C. 2024. *A Woman Is a School.* New York: Slow Factory Press.

Chapter 11

Capital, Hope, and "A Moment of Terrible Social Intensity": A Conversation with John Holloway[1]

Matt Meyer and Suren Moodliar, June 11, 2021

As 2020 drew to a close, the Movements of Movements project, which grew out of a left circle connected to the World Social Forum, convened a series of conversations about the challenges and opportunities facing the left.[1] During a year with few historical parallels and to better understand the conjuncture, two project members, Moodliar and Meyer, reached out to John Holloway, who has devoted a considerable amount of work to understanding the relationship between the rule of capital and the grounds for hope. In the resulting interview, one that takes a conceptual turn, a series of distinctions are evoked to clarify the contradictions that emerge in practice—social movements versus movements-in-opposition, the working class versus the proletariat, "the end of

1 This interview was published as an open-source, online article in CounterPunch.org: https://www.counterpunch.org. It took place on June 11, 2021, and can be accessed here: https://www.counterpunch.org/2021/06/11/capital-hope-and-a-moment-of-terrible-social-intensity-a-conversation-with-john-holloway/

history" versus "shattering the continuum of history," state violence versus righteous rage, capital, and hope.

Born in Dublin, resident in Mexico City, Holloway is best known as a movement thinker who has grappled with the theory of state in capitalism and has gone on to help us understand the meaning and potential of global movements to transcend the rule of capital. Meyer, a resident of Brooklyn, is a lifelong activist, author, and educator working within the black liberation and global peace movements. South African-born Moodliar is managing editor of *Socialism and Democracy* and a Boston-based activist.[2]

Suren Moodliar: *We'll have several detours in the conversation along the way to hope, but our starting point has to be* Change the World Without Taking Power.[3] *It is no exaggeration to call it "a seminal text." It inspired activists, provoked a whole seminar series, generated counter books, and prompted many repetitions of the phrase, "change the world without...." Can you take us back to the context in which you wrote that book?*

John Holloway: The moment in which it came out was pretty important. The book itself was something that I had been working on for years. I was involved in the old debates of the Conference of Socialist Economists in Britain, in the '70s and '80s, around the state, and really developing the idea, which also connected with the German State Derivation Debate.[4] So the central question there was how we understand the state as a *capitalist* state. If we understand the state as a capitalist state, then it seemed to me obvious that means we can't think of changing the world through the state. I just took that for granted as being obvious.

By the time I finally formulated all this into a book, it was 2002—a very lively time. Especially in Latin America, especially in Argentina. The book was published in Spanish in Argentina, just after the uprising of December 2001 and the whole movement that stretched into 2002. So it just connected perfectly there with all the discussions that were going on, and also connected obviously with the whole Zapatista and post-Zapatista *alter-globalization* movement.

In that sense, the timing was very fortunate, I think. And partly because of that, it sparked off loads and loads of discussions. It was translated into eleven languages, I think. When I first finished the book, I thought, "Well, maybe a few of my friends will understand what I'm trying to say." But the reaction was just fantastic.

Suren: *I appreciate the context of the alter-globalization movement, events in Argentina, and so on. But this was also the time when the Pink Tide seemed to be coming in. There were many state-based projects, including most spectacularly, the Bolivarian project in Venezuela, one that seemed very credible. What was the chemistry between these two—those taking power and those seeking change without taking power?*

John: I think with Venezuela there really was not so much of a connection. My contact in Venezuela is the absolutely fabulous cooperative known as CECOSESOLA [*Central de las cooperativas de Lara*, Cooperatives of Social Services of Lara State], which has existed for nearly fifty years. They are a center of cooperatives and their main activity is what they call, peculiarly, "a festival of consumption." But their festival is actually the organization of a popular supermarket each weekend, where food is provided to the community. This is in the town of Barquisimeto—a huge proportion of the town's population go there every week.

The amazing thing is that if you go there and visit them, you discover that they spend a big part of their time just sitting around in circles, with children. They discuss their problems, personal problems, communal problems. And in this way, they're trying to build a different world.

Their argument, which was really a critical argument already at that time of the Bolivarian government, was that "if you really want to change things, you can't just bring in a decree that now there are going to be lots of cooperatives." You need a process of years and years of work together, developing different social relations, different ways of doing things, different ways of thinking about things.

I suppose the three things that had a big impact in Latin America were the whole movement in Argentina, which was just amazing, the War of Water in Bolivia in the 2000, and—all the time—the background of the Zapatista movement here in Mexico, which has just been an amazing source of inspiration.

Matt Meyer: *I'm curious as to whether you've had contact with the folks in Venezuela who helped develop the First Eco-Socialist International. I am not aware of them particularly citing you, but there's no question that part of the conversations among the eco-socialists has been along similar lines. Obviously in Venezuela they have a Ministry of Eco-socialism, but those who founded the International are grassroots folks who led the movement to get rid of Monsanto, as well as the movement being called "Trueke"—bartering and trade—mainly rooted in the Afro-Venezuelan centers of the country.*

It seems to me fairly inevitable that some of the concepts that you have put forward, like the idea of ceasing to "create" capitalism, are integrated into that mindset, whether because of an overt understanding of those concepts or just because of the evolutionary way in which it's become clear that the state is not necessarily the only, or perhaps the major, way of making revolution.

Social Movements versus Movements in Opposition

Suren: *To follow up on that, you famously challenged the idea of social movements as an emancipatory category, preferring instead the idea of "movements-in-opposition." You've described the anti-privatization water movement in Bolivia in very positive terms. Can you say a little bit more about the distinction between social movements and the oppositional movements?*

John: It is not so much a distinction. There's a question of vocabulary in conceptualization. It's really in the last twenty to thirty years that the notion of social movements has arisen. And I think to some extent, initially it was a conscious attempt to get away from the language of class struggle. This may be wrong, but the idea of the social movements suggests an infinite number of movements struggling against particular injustices.

But the peculiar thing is that if you've got an infinite or this huge number of disparate movements, then you're in fact killing the notion of hope. Because [these movements form] a permanent thing. Of course, you're going to win one struggle, lose another. You'll lose most of them and you'll win some of them, and it'll go on and on. There is no longer any revolutionary perspective. There's no longer any perspective, except in the most general terms. There's no direct fighting against capitalism as a coherent social system.

If you look at all of these movements, they're not *social*. I mean, they're social movements in one sense, but they're actually movements of resistance. They are movements that arise from some sort of aggression, which can be understood normally as a capitalist depression. So they are in fact movements of resistance, and in the best, most active cases, they're movements of resistance and rebellion. What really annoys me is the degree to which this notion of social movements has become established: convenient enough, but actually very destructive, both theoretically and politically.

Suren: *If one looks at Alain Touraine's overall trajectory, he first began to write extensively about social movements after looking at the 1968 student movements, and then discovered movements like Solidarity in Poland or the Corsican nationalist movement. In that period, he also developed the idea of the sociological intervention, in which he brought together movement activists of various parts of the movement, and seemed to have an intuition that by understanding the interaction between the activists in different parts of the movement, we get an overall sense of their developmental potential and their transformational capacity.*

Of course, by the late 1990s, he almost arrives at the end of history, and as you say, at the end of hope. So I find your argument about the way in which social movements were conceptualized very helpful. Although I do want to recognize that there are many sociologists who still use the vocabulary and see it in emancipatory terms as well.

John: That's right. It's quite difficult to avoid the vocabulary completely, and of course, as you're saying, many sociologists and students do want to do something radical. The easiest way to think about it is that if we focus solely on social movements, something important is lost.

Suren: *This brings me to another dichotomy, the proletariat against the working class. Can you tell us a little bit about that?*

John: I take this from Katherina Nasioka, a PhD student of mine whose thesis was later published as a book. She focused on the uprising in Oaxaca in 2006, and the uprising in Athens, and

Greece as a whole, in 2010. She's Greek herself and her argument is that the best way to understand what was happening is as a result of the proletariat against the working class.[5]

If you look at Greece, especially at that time, there were very big conflicts within the radical left. There are few who don't want to be called left, the radical anticapitalists or rebels on the one hand, and the powerful structure of the trade unions, still dominated by the old Communist Party, on the other.

In that context, I remember there was one occasion in 2011 when the organized workers, the "working class" in that sense, actually physically defended the Parliament from an assault by the rebels. I have another Greek former PhD student, Panagiotis Doulos, who says that we probably shouldn't attach the name "rebels" to the opposition. We should think of them as some "movement without name" against the organized and named working class.

"A Moment of Terrible Social Intensity"

Matt: *It seems to me we're stuck in some ways, in part, in the naming of things. Because parts of what they're talking about are old left versus new left and newer left. Some of this may just be different ways of attacking the problem. But part of it is a conceptual one: whether social movements can be a form building more radical or revolutionary movements.*

As we've talked about the "end of history" and the end of hope, you've written about "shattering the continuum of history," which I think is a much more interesting concept. In fact, it's not about the end of history, it's about the end of conceptualizing things in a particular way, especially about (re)creating capitalism in a particular way and replacing it with something else.

John, you've written some years ago that we want a moment or we need a moment of terrible social intensity. Are we at that moment today? Have we reached that moment? If we have, if this is that moment, then what do people need to be doing to shatter the continuum of history and build new forms?

John: The easy answer is I don't know!

I would say we're possibly on the edge of such a moment. Okay, this is silly, but you remember the musical *West Side Story* and the song "Something's Coming!"? It's only at the beginning, but kind of on the edge. Something's going to happen, maybe something good, but we don't know what.

I think there are moments when you can actually feel that. In Argentina in December 2001, you could really feel kind of an excitement and tension and anger in the air. I also happened to be in Athens in 2011, just before the occupation of the squares began. Are we in that moment now? It is always fairly hard to judge. What I would say is that yes, but probably not within a week.

I think that it is very likely, or very possible rather, that within one or two years, we will be in a really explosive situation in different parts of the world. And I suspect different cities of the world in particular. I think that we're in a situation of suspense at the moment. It's just not clear how things are going to come out. It's not just the US; it's not clear what's going to happen with the whole situation of capitalism in the next couple of years.

One real possibility is that we're in a situation rather like the 1930s, but possibly much worse. We might see a period of huge unemployment, of real impoverishment, of growing nationalism, of a growing push toward the possibility of war. How do we prepare for that? How do we think of that? That's really the question you're posing.

I suppose in terms of anger, there's kind of a reasoning that says we should win periods of great anger, but there are also historical experiences which suggest that we tend to lose in periods of great anger. If we think obviously of the 1930s, but also just back to 2008 and all that followed, I think that led to a huge upsurge in social anger throughout the world. But that social anger was then expressed in the rise of people like Trump, Johnson, or Bolsonaro.

It may be that what's going to happen... is a surge of social anger. How do we say that this anger is ours? Is it anger against capital? This anger has to come in our direction.... How do we intervene in an angry world?

It may be that what's going to happen over the next couple of years is a similar and much greater surge of social anger. How do we say that *this anger is ours*? Is it anger against capital? This anger has to come in our direction. How do we do that? How do we intervene in an angry world, an angry and also fairly diffuse world? I don't have a clear answer at all. Obviously we try to make the connections between people's anger and the failure of capital. I suppose that is what's happening at the moment, in a way, with the pandemic.

But it seems really important to say: "Look, this is the failure of a system." It's the failure of capitalism, that's what we're living now. Lots of people are saying that I suppose, but how do we use that, and think in terms of change through that. Obviously, I don't think it's a question of electoral politics. Maybe one could use some electoral politics in terms of opposing things, but not in terms of proposing things.

Matt: *As part of reconceptualizing and rethinking or rebuilding revolution, are there ways that blow apart old and sometimes false dichotomies? Are there tactical, strategic, and sometimes philosophical* *conceptions of violence and nonviolence, for example, that need to be reworked, the idea of only being able to make revolution one way and not the other. How can we not get stuck in dogmas, in old dichotomies, possibly like violence/nonviolence.*

The recent piece that you wrote about the world post-COVID speaks a little bit to hope beyond the current crises.[6] *Part of what you wrote says: "Well, what do we do with the capitalists? Maybe we should just hang them by the nearest lamppost. Or maybe just forget about them. Yeah, better to just forget about them." What is your thinking about getting past these dichotomies?*

John: I'd forgotten about that thing! But yes, people got annoyed with that.

I think it's what I was saying a moment ago. We have to start from or at least certainly respect people's anger. The Zapatistas have this fantastic phrase, *La Digna Rabia*—Righteous rage! And that seems to me absolutely the right way to think about it. We have to think of change, we have to think of movements, not starting from rational argument but in terms of respect for the anger that people feel.

From that anger, I suppose my feeling is that the best way, without wanting to be completely pacifist, would be to say that violence seemed to be a mistake. It was and is the wrong way to express our anger for two reasons.

Firstly, because we're just not very good at it! We're not violent people. If I took up and matched guns against the Mexican state, obviously I would lose. I mean, it'd be ridiculous.

And the other thing is that it's not part of the society we want to create. Whereas I wouldn't rush to condemn somebody for being violent—it's not a kind of principled pacifism—but the important thing really is to find how to express our anger in dignified, worthy, righteous ways. And that is something else. That is not shooting people, and it is not hitting people.

Capital & Identity

Suren: *John, you have also considered the challenge of identity politics. Respect and dignity are at the core of this form of politics. In talking about "a many-headed Hydra," which expresses itself in the traditional race, class, and gender kinds of distinctions, you've written that we need to go back to the notion of capital and see it as a transitory phenomenon. How may we conceptualize capital in order to transcend it and how this relates to your critique of identity?*

John: This really goes back to my involvement in the state derivation debate in the 1970s. The question there really was: how do we derive the particularization of the state from the nature of capitalist social relations? In other words, the question is, how do we derive the existence of the political as something distinct from the economic? How do we conceptualize this from the base, from the nature of capitalist social relations? That leads us then to the idea that capital is characterized by this separation into the political and the economic. In other words, when we are talking about capital, we're talking about the totality of social relations.

Capital is not just an economic category. It's a way of talking about the totality of social obligations and saying that this totality of social relations has a certain structure, a certain form. This is how Marx analyzes things in *Capital*. It's based on the fact that richness or wealth exists in the form of commodities. When I talk about the importance of capital, I'm not talking just about the importance of the economic, okay? There is importance in trying to understand the structure and dynamic of social relations in society.

If we lose the overall concept of capital, if everything dissolves into a multitude of social movements, then the idea of a fundamental transformation of society gets lost completely.

Secondly, what I've been thinking more and more about over the past year or so is that this concept of capital is crucial for thinking about hope. We tend to think of capital as a form of domination, which of course it is. But the idea of an overall structure of society is crucial for thinking about hope. We need this in order to understand that, yes, we really can transform society as a whole. If we lose the overall concept of capital, if everything dissolves into a multitude of social movements, then the idea of a fundamental transformation of society gets lost completely. And I think that is what's been happening with many contemporary protest movements.

There is a loss of the concept of capital. There are fewer and fewer students reading *Capital*, for example. Fewer are understanding or using that language. It may be that more students are working on social movements, or women's movements, or studying gender; I don't know. But there is a loss of this overall concept of a social structure that can be transformed.

Identity comes into it because I think that these losses are part of the growth of particularistic politics, divorced from some sort of conception of a universal or totalizing structure. Whereas if we think about political capital, then we're thinking of society as being antagonistic, constitutively antagonistic, to things that don't penetrate into all of us. If political capital penetrates into all of us, then it's silly to think that we have some sort of identity separated from that antagonism. Does that make sense?

Matt: *I think it's not a coincidence that these contradictions have emerged so strikingly at a time when we talk a lot about the nonprofit industrial complex, the "professionalization" of social* *change. We talk a lot more about social change and a lot more about individualized or personalized depression, and a lot less about revolution—a lot less about liberation.*

John: I think that's right.

Dual Power

Suren: *In thinking about how we oppose Capital as a whole, you've proposed antipower. Where does the historical notion of dual power fit in, if at all? In other words, how can we go about building another form of power within the capitalist society, in order to transcend it?*

John: You're asking where the notion of dual power fits in?

The notion of dual power, I suppose, is usually associated with the traditional state-centered idea of revolutions. It's a situation of dual power in Russia in 1917, no? How should we think about it at this moment? I suppose, I don't know. If we're talking about cracks, for example, then we have to talk about the development of more and more attempts to create spaces or times that go against capital. There are different ways of developing things. Do you call that a situation of dual power? Perhaps.

Suren: *My question is a bit of an anachronism in that we hardly talk about dual power anymore. However, there are many projects, especially here in the United States, that don't quite reject electoral politics but are involved in building regional networks and systems of power, as it were. There is some coordination between political projects and more community-based cooperatives, like Cooperation Jackson or Cooperation Humboldt.*

John: I think that these questions are definitely important. It connects with something that we've been discussing here—the increasing use of alternatives. But in Mexico and Latin America, instead of talking about revolution, people are talking about the construction of alternatives. The construction of alternatives obviously could be seen in terms of dual power. And when we go on creating alternatives, we are creating a different world.

On the one hand, I find the growth of all these movements trying to do things in a different way quite exciting. But I also find it disturbing in the sense that some of these are not actually alternatives at all. But some of what is developing are in fact movements against capitalist organization or capitalist imposition. We have to theorize this way and understand a certain negative grammar. Negative grammar may say, okay, these are exciting movements, but they're movements against—movements against capital, rather than just movements for the creation of something else. We must wonder, why? Why insist on this negative grammar?

I think it's a little bit like raising a flag. What are we trying to do? If we're writing a thesis or a book, if we're organizing around something, we want to raise a black and red flag on top of it! Sometimes we don't want to say it and sometimes it doesn't make sense to say it. But perhaps it's important for us to at least have that flag in our minds!

I suppose that comes back to the question of dual power. We must understand dual power as part of a fundamental antagonism, and not just the proliferation of different things. Because the proliferation of different things is fairly easily integrate-able back into capital.

Suren: *So we must keep in mind the idea of a break; the antagonism has to be central even when deploying the euphemistic term "alternative"?*

John: I think so, yes. It's a kind of protection, giving "alternatives" some clear direction against capital.

Suren: *Against the totalization of capital, you're proposing "many worlds." How are these many worlds supposed to relate to one another? What are the forms of communication and negotiation that have to happen between these many worlds?*

John: It's not me who's proposing the many worlds, it's the Zapatistas who say "we want to create a world of many worlds." And the Zapatistas are extremely important in all these discussions. This growth of emphasis on alternatives, for example—certainly in Latin America—is very much connected with Indigenous movements. But the way I understand the Zapatistas is that they are saying "absolutely not." We are anticapitalist. They're far too diplomatic and far too clever to simply say "we are not an alternative." But especially with the EZLN Sixth Declaration in 2005, they say explicitly for the first time: "We are Anti-Capitalist."[7]

There are two new communiqués that came out in October 2020 that are absolutely astonishing, brilliant. They're saying: look, we're going to go to all the continents of the world, to set sail in April. This isn't a question of an Indigenous movement, they assert. We need every color, every people from all over the world to think about breaking with the catastrophe that we're living. It seems to me they're breaking completely with this kind of "alternative" picture.[8]

The Zapatista idea of a world of many worlds is terrific but it's not *now*. In order to get to the world of many worlds, we have to break with a single capitalist imposition of a logic of destruction. We must think about how we would organize or build organization and interconnection between different worlds or different communities. This thinking and organizing may be growing, with many different experiments. But some things will have to be left for when it comes.

Hope

Matt: *So what should we do now, as we look toward the edge of the cliff we're on now?*

John: I am trying to write a book on hope. My starting point in all this was Ernst Bloch's *Principle of Hope*,[9] which took me into Marx and all the discussions. He starts off saying that when he comes back to Germany after the war, after exile in the States, that now is the time to learn hope. My argument is that in this situation, we are again in a time to learn hope. We're no longer in the same context as Bloch. He was still thinking in terms of a traditional concept of revolution led by the Communist Party. Today, there aren't any significant revolutionary parties in the world. Things seem to be getting darker and darker in many ways.

And yet there's a real need for hope.

People actually relate to this idea all the time. It's the one cliche that is used by every single politician. For us, the only way we can think about hope is by thinking about the crisis of capital, the crisis of the existing system. How do we connect hope to our notion of the crisis, and what this crisis means?

We want to think of hope in relation to the crisis. There has to be some way in which a breakdown of the system is part of the transition to a different world. I think possibly that's what we're living or what we're going to be living in the next few years. We must figure out how to think about this in a way that isn't Armageddonist. It does seem to me likely that we will be in a social crisis within a year or two that we just have no experience of. We don't really have a clear conception of what it might mean politically and socially to have that level of great crisis in the current world. On the one hand, that prospect is very frightening but, on the other hand, perhaps not. Perhaps we have to think of hope in that context.

NOTES

1. "Movements of Movements Conversations," The Movements of Movements Project, accessed May 13, 2021, https://movementsofmovements.net/movement-spaces/conversations. ↑
2. Matt Meyer is Co-Secretary General of the International Peace Research Association. Suren Moodliar is a coordinator of *encuentro5*, a Boston-based movement-building center. ↑
3. John Holloway, *Change the World Without Taking Power* (London and Ann Arbor, MI: Pluto Press, 2005). ↑
4. John Holloway and Sol Picciotto, eds., *State and Capital: A Marxist Debate* (London: Edward Arnold, 1978). ↑
5. John Holloway, Katerina Nasiōka, and Panagiōtēs Doulos, eds., *Beyond Crisis: After the Collapse of Institutional Hope in Greece, What?* (Oakland, CA: PM Press, 2020). ↑
6. John Holloway, "A Cascade of Angers—My COVID 19 Fantasy," *Daraja Press* (blog), June 17, 2020, https://darajapress.com/2020/06/17/john-holloway-a-cascade-of-angers-my-covid-19-fantasy. ↑
7. "Sixth Declaration of the Selva Lacandona," Enlace Zapatista (blog), May 10, 2010, https://enlacezapatista.ezln.org.mx/sdsl-en. ↑

8. "Sexta parte: Una Montaña en Alta Mar," Enlace Zapatista (blog), October 5, 2020, http://enlacezapatista.ezln.org.mx/2020/10/05/sexta-parte-una-montana-en-alta-mar. ↑
9. Ernst Bloch, *The Principle of Hope*, 1. MIT paperback ed. (Cambridge, MA: MIT Press, [1954] 1995). ↑

Chapter 12

Beyond Our Mythologized Histories: A Word About Violence, Nonviolence, and Nuance

Too much has been written about what I've termed the false dichotomies between "nonviolence" and "violence." Several of us have asserted that we will "refuse to choose" between those often-cited "opposites" of the 1960s US-based Black liberation movements: Rev. Dr. Martin Luther King, Jr., and Minister Malcolm X/El Hajj-Malik el-Shabazz. There are plenty of books in print now to document how both of those iconic leaders were drawing closer to one another's global viewpoints.

As they aged and matured, they readied for the assassin's bullet, which both expected was inevitable given their political trajectories in the context of US racist-capitalist-imperialism. And that was only 1965-1968!

Fast forward sixty years and taken from a worldwide, movement-building viewpoint, the discussions, arguments, and splits regarding strategies and tactics seem as contentious as ever—especially in the Global North, and especially among the *least* oppressed: white folks, academics and activists alike, who work overtime to prove their points that only one method of struggle will take the collected masses to the revolution—nonviolent or armed. Many seem to have conveniently forgotten that Minister Malcolm spoke eloquently of the need to struggle "by any means necessary"—not by only one or two means and no others.

A quick review of recent literature on one side or the other of these debates reveals more of an invisibilizing effect than outright lying or overt distortion. Except for the subtitle "forcing nonviolence on forgetful movements," I was pleased to read Peter Gelderloos's new book, *They Will Beat the Memory Out of Us* (Pluto Press, 2024),[2] because it avoided some of these oversimplifications that I criticized in a review essay of an earlier book of his. The idea that there are and have been no nonviolent activists committed to revolutionary social change is as much a distortion as the idea that the majority of armed combatants of radical people's movements over the past century were proponents of violence rather than propagators of peace. As I said in a tribute to Black Liberation Army elder and dear friend Sekou Odinga at the African Peace Studies Conference African Liberation Day celebration held in Tanzania, "Sekou has been called by many 'our General,' which is appropriate. But he was also calling for us to settle our differences and find more reasons to unite than subdivide and was thus also one of our greatest peacemakers."

Bill Sutherland, Barbara Deming, Dave Dellinger, Rosa Parks, Ella Baker, and so many others were, to use the self-describing term coined by feminist poet Grace Paley, US-born "combative pacifists." Some would suggest that they weren't pacifists at all. Indeed, the differences between that word, the phrase "nonviolent activist," and others are all muddied in the 21st-century context of

---

2 Gelderloos, P. *They Will Beat the Memory Out of Us: Forcing Nonviolence on Forgetful Movements.* Pluto Press, 2024.

liberatory paradigms. We need desperately to break out of simple, old-fashioned, ideas of single-tactic, single-strategy, "this way to win" tomfoolery.

Amilcar Cabral, Thomas Sankara, Graca Machel, Kwame Nkrumah, Julius Nyerere, and many more were staunch supporters of armed struggle against colonialism and oppression but were also dedicated antimilitarists, peacemakers, and supporters of nonviolent direct action. Amina of Zazzau, whose cartoon image is one of those less-known figures whose face graces the cover of this book, was a 16th-century freedom fighter Queen who led her people (and army) to fortify and defend their Hausa territory. Though some accounts suggest a focus on militaristic tendencies, her main legacy in modern-day Nigeria is that she was clearly as capable as any man in all aspects of public life. Wampanoag sachem (chief) Weetamoo, also pictured on the cover, was more known for her peacemaking diplomacy than her role in the land-grabbing King Philip's War—but her leadership in all areas was recognized by her ascendency as representative of all allied tribes within the Wampanoag Confederation.

Perhaps the most mythologized histories along the violence/nonviolence "divide" involve another face on the cover: Nobel Peace laureate Archbishop Desmond Tutu, along with Nelson Mandela and the South African anti-apartheid struggle in general. Whole books have been written extolling the extraordinary virtues of the successful nonviolent campaigns responsible for an end to the racist regime, books which fit uncomfortably on the shelves alongside of the books written describing the triumphant armed struggle that defeated apartheid rule! In this Orwellian confusion, Nelson Mandela is made out to be a great proponent of nonviolence, and, in turn, Winnie Mandela is made out to be a terrorist advocate of vicious acts of violence—mainly perpetrated against fellow African peoples. Arch Tutu, somewhere in the middle, gets saintly status similar to Martin Luther King or Gandhi: those who could do no wrong in their righteous efforts to free their people.

The more complicated truth is that Nelson could have gotten out of prison many years, before he did had he only renounced the armed struggle and called for peaceful negotiations in the 1970s or '80s. Winnie helped hold together a sometimes-fragile unity among fighting factions of the liberation movement, forever a symbol of a powerful woman who was most inclined to self-sacrifice for the liberation cause. And Archbishop Tutu remained true to his Black Consciousness, Biko-trained roots—ready to give support to sometimes unpopular causes, like the release of political prisoners such as the aforementioned Sekou Odinga. Tutu was the leading voice among South Africans calling the Zionist settler colonial regime "apartheid," stating that modern Israeli apartheid was, if anything, worse than what the Africans in his homeland suffered. None of these figures got everything right or took the best possible position on every issue. But all of them understood the nuanced realities of fighting a contemporary struggle using "any means necessary": favoring peaceful means and nonviolence as much as possible but allowing for armed self-defense and liberation struggles as needed.

But John Holloway, in many ways, a visionary for his decision (as an older European scholar) to put his lot in with the Zapatistas and other movements of Latin America, says that while he is "not completely pacifist" he leans heavily in that direction. When Holloway states that in his opinion violence is a mistake, he suggests that the movements of people against capitalism throughout history that have included radical armed components, have all been wrong. The entire history of the Cuban revolution, warts and all, the attempts to make Vietnam "ten times more beautiful" following decades of French and US imperial aggression, and the successful Mozambican struggle for independence, all contradict—in sharp historical contrast—this "nonviolent narrative."

Even the Zapatista decision to cease the armed struggle in southern Mexico was done so at the point where they were deciding both to expand their political reach beyond their territories as well as to maintain their arms for the defense of Chiapas and beyond. At the heart of any discussion about creating movements that confront capital is always the inherent violence of the barbaric extractive system. Whatever tactical decisions are made in a given locale or historical context, the sacrifices made in these struggles—including the mistakes within—are nevertheless never, as Holloway also suggests, "ridiculous." Though there continue to be "ridiculous" mistakes made on both sides of the nonviolence-armed struggle divide, for those in all camps working to eradicate the roots of oppression, more respectful language and communication must be developed.

Gelderloos, in this regard, is very correct in his summary of Mariame Kaba and Andrea Ritchie: "If we are to have any hope," he writes, "we need to see how self-defense, survival, healing, and compassion actually require the same kind of transformations from us."[3] These words are a direct counterpoint to absolute pacifisms, which have paternalistically and opportunistically undermined people's struggles for decades. Criticizing Palestinian youth for throwing rocks at armed tanks is not an assertion of the power of nonviolence, it is an only-slightly-veiled apology for genocide. While it must be noted that many in the war resistance and radical nonviolence movements have long made a distinction between

3 Gelderloos, 2024, p. 137.

their solidarity work and the dogmatic approaches to absolute nonviolence, there are still lingering assumptions that sometimes get in the way. Paul and Mark Engler have done a masterful job at popularizing some old ideas in their *This Is an Uprising: How Nonviolent Revolt Is Shaping the 21st Century* (Bold Type Books, 2016), and they have spotlighted how theorists like Gene Sharp have distinguished between strategic nonviolence and the moral pacifism that Sharp himself disliked.[4] There is still too much of a mixing of the data provided by political scientist Erica Chenoweth and others, however, whose research about the success rates of nonviolent direct action was never meant to be taken as an ideological or dogmatic mantra that nowadays nonviolence always works and armed struggle is a dead end.

Mozambique's own nonviolent histories must be taken side by side with the victory of their armed struggle. Their post-independence issues with a protracted contra war and subsequent youth violence must be seen in direct relief alongside Graca Machel and others' championing of the rights of youth to be free from all forms of violence and the pioneering work to end the callous use of child soldiers in all arenas of conflict.[5] That all this comes out of one southern African country is no coincidence, filled with many mistakes along the way, but also with so much creative building for new futures.

All of history asserts—and Peace Research and Study (especially from the South) demands—that the time is over for past

---

4 Engler, M. "A History of Nonviolence," from https://democracyuprising.com/2006/09/13/a-history-of-nonviolence/, Accessed 25 November 2024.

5 Meyer, M. "Mozambique: Liberation Myths and Nonviolent Strategies," in Bartkowski, M. *Recovering Nonviolent History: Civil Resistance in Liberation Struggle*. Lynne Reinner, 2013.

simplifications and mythologies designed to serve the long-term interests of capital or even the short-term interests of past revolutionaries who thought they had all the answers. Though those two groups were indeed very different, with different motivations, interests, and power, for those looking to continue building a path toward human rights and a sustainable future for all, we must embrace the nuances that sometimes seem contradictory. We must move beyond our grandfather's sectarian battles, talk tactically and strategically across past divisions, and build a new world based on science and sweat.

Chapter 13

Africa World Peace: A Book Series and an Ideal

When Kassahun Checole initiated the proposal that the time was ripe for a new Africa World Press/Red Sea Press book series and imprint, it was largely in recognition of the growth of the field of African Peace Studies outlined herein. Our first task was to set parameters for such a series, which we wrote as summary, preamble, and mission statement as follows:

Africa World Press & Red Sea Press (AWP/RSP) are launching a new series of books on Peace, Social Change, and Reconciliation. This new series will focus on the study and practice of peacebuilding, the carceral state, human rights, nonviolent resistance, social change, and people's movements throughout the Global South and the Diaspora.

Preamble:

As the last half of the last century introduced a surge of social change centered around what Mwalimu Julius Nyerere called "flag independence," the unfinished international project of total decolonization found a myriad of strategies, ideologies, and processes for transforming societies in radical and liberating ways. The first quarter of this century saw shifts such that research on "peace"—the absence of conflict without necessarily the presence of justice—became central to new, interdisciplinary writings about nonviolence, resolution of armed conflicts, personal communications, and mediation. Today, the world faces an ever-maturing academic field of African peace studies. Activist struggles and organizing for long-term movement-building against militarism, oppression, and continuing colonial/neo-colonial imperial adventures challenge our collective strategic thinking about work, the world around us, and life itself. AWP/RSP's new book series will produce books and other educational materials to spotlight cutting-edge developments in all these areas of study, organizing, everyday resistance, and struggles for social change.

Mission Statement:

Beginning in 2025, AWP/RSP will focus on producing a series of books and educational products, single-authored or edited, focusing on current issues related to peoples' struggles for human rights and social change through citizen activism and struggle. The books will be as intentionally interdisciplinary as appropriate and will include scholarship from historians, philosophers, political scientists, political economists, sociologists, and many others—including community-based narratives that are based on grassroots wisdom and especially Indigenous knowledge. They will include studies on social movements that focus on human rights, on climate change, and on the interaction between socio-political local and regional efforts against monopolies, bad governance, and empire. Some of the issues we will cover will spotlight movements focusing on women's liberation, on prison reform and abolition, on climate crisis and opportunities, on war and justice, and the overall impact of the military-prison-industrial complex. In addition to traditional academic books, we will produce materials in other mediums including graphic novels and comic books, young adult and children's picture books, and virtual web-based materials.

Our goals, therefore, as the previous chapters in this short, first book in the series outline, extend well beyond the continent of Africa and well beyond traditional notions of "conflict resolution." With a distinguished Editorial Board—including scholars and grassroots rabble-rousers; parliamentarians and vice chancellors; folks associated with Nobel Peace, MBE, and other high-level recognitions and accreditations; rebellious students and precocious youth—we look forward to our work together building networks between us and producing tools for advanced study and struggle. Our operational bases will be in New York, Oxford, and various locales throughout the African continent.

It is clear that Africa will be our focus and centering point, but not our exclusive lens through which to view the world or the words we'll use.

It is clear that we intend to emphasize the main trends of social change and peacemaking that seem most urgent as well as useful at this time. It is clear that our politics are broad, inclusive, embracing, and nondogmatic, and that the authors we will seek and accept will have strong principles and visions, but not beliefs that any one of them have all the answers to all the major questions of our day.

**

We are rooted in an understanding that there are new paradigms and concrete practices[1] being developed, researched, and utilized—and many more in need of support and engagement — to protect all the peoples of the world, creating human security, environmental growth (and degrowth), and justice for all. We understand that time is long up for the short-sided world view that "the enemy of my enemy is my friend," preferring instead to delve deeply into the thinking behind the "three-way-fight" politics opposing fascism and building movement based on life-affirming truth-telling.[2] We are inspired by the things that challenge us and are challenged to understand better and replicate the things that inspire us. Thus we appreciate new juxtaposed concepts, like the "ubuntu for warriors," which intentionally calls out, subversively, to "refuse to descend into worshiping war and violence."[3]

We appreciate the way eco-feminist Ayisha Siddiqa asks: "What if the future is soft and revolution is so kind that there is no end to us in sight?... Love is still the only revenge. It grows each time the earth is set on fire."

We are impatient that the fire next time, and the one after that, did not burn down the systems that continue to oppress. And we are worried about the water, which seems to be getting more and more commodified as every bit of space and resource is made into

---

1 We purposefully use this phrasing in homage to one hopeful space based on study and practice: Furnari, E., Janzen, R., and Kabaki, R. 2023. *Unarmed Civilian Protection: A New Paradigm for Protection and Human Security.* Bristol: Bristol University Press.

2 For inspiration here, see: Alexander, X., and Lyons, M. (eds.). 2024. *Three Way Fight: Revolutionary Politics and Antifascism*. Oakland and Montreal: PM Press/Kersplebedeb.

3 Chasi, C. 2021. *Ubuntu for Warriors.* Trenton: Africa World Press.

another "new and improved" product. But we are committed to fighting against the scourge of war and all the causes of war, through our bodies, our lives, our voices, our words, the power of our pens and the movements we will build with them. We are hopeful that our scientific research and validated studies of a decolonized, justice-filled peace will lead to informed organizing for international people's power such that the Earth has heretofore never seen.

We reach out, beyond the boundaries, past border walls and passport checkpoints, to reach that horizon where we see, feel, smell, taste, breathe, hug, and love PEACE.

Acknowledgments

The vision and reality of this book and this book series would not have been possible on any level without the profound and sustained leadership and hard work of Africa World Press CEO, and also someone I am proud to call Brother, Kassahun Checole. The entire Kassahun family, and especially Ayo, brighten our lives as well as our shared world. This book is also unthinkable without the copy-editing prowess of the amazing Betsy Mickel. Without her, many silly errors and confusing sentences would be present; any remaining errors in wording or clarity are my own.

The vision and reality of my thinking and actions about most things in life—especially regarding peace and social change—are based primarily on the teaching of my three great mentors, mentioned throughout this book: Pan Africanists Bill Sutherland and Mawina Kouyate, and Afro-Puerto Rican renaissance man Luis Nieves Falcon. The inclusion of Dr. Nieves Falcon's smile on the cover of this book is just one way of paying homage to the Afro-Puerto Rican comrade who would become my son's godfather; the praxis of his strategic analysis, writings, thinking, action, commitment, love of culture, and organizational sense guides so much of my political work today.

The problem with Acknowledgments is the inevitability that someone(s) will be left out, so let's be clear that there are many who had a hand in the ideas in this book, with apologies to all those not named below. Special mention must be made to the ever-inspiring work of Nozizwe Madlala-Routledge, Silvia Federici, and

Diana Marcela Agudelo-Ortiz, each of whom graciously provided endorsements of this book and who also provide so much more than that to me, personally and politically. My comrade, another Brother, Jihad Abdulmumit, gives me reason to think and rethink my work in the USA—one of the few who makes me consider that the land of my birth might still be worth fighting for, for justice for all. His leadership and friendship are two sides of my reality that make it possible to breathe in the spaces of a dying empire. So many others in the Black liberation movement and the Puerto Rican movement provide additional room to explore, to study, to struggle, and to rebuild, so I'll just shout out my comrades in the Spirit of Mandela Coalition, the National Boricua Human Rights Network, and all the recently released and especially still-incarcerated political prisoners. As a person of similar ethnic and socio-cultural background, David Gilbert has helped me think humbly about keeping the work and the faith going for the long-term, so beyond these names—and with the hope that even more political prisoners will gain freedom from the time I type this to the time it gets printed and read, I'll simply say: FREE ALL POLITICAL PRISONERS EVERYWHERE!

My recent academic work has almost all been done in the context of the International Peace Research Association. In those and related spaces, it is important to note my partnerships with Maria Teresa Munoz, Frances Peterson, Christine Atieno, Vidya Jain, Rajib Tamilsina, Kelli Te Maihāroa, Hakim Williams, Akilah Jaramogi, Michael Loadenthal, Roy Tamashiro, Mark Lance, Polly Walker, Wim Lavin, Charles Wasike, Moses Monday, Elavie Ndura, and Liz Carmichael. In the circle of Resistance Studies, I acknowledge with a warm hug my Brother Stellen Vinhagen (for an only child, I do have a lot of siblings!). Mandy Carter, Amilar Shabazz,

Artemis Duffy, the Movements of Movements gang, Kali Akuno, Saki Hall, and actual biological relative Diane Lehrenbaum (plus her sons) are pushing their way into my mind at the moment! The entire UK team at Oxford, under the leadership of Abebe Zegeye, have already provided ideas and support that have made their ways into this work. Our plans for future work help provide the drive for what is still to come.

In the space between the personal and the political, the concrete building blocks of everyday revolution, survival, and sustainability there are Michael and Molly. Also, in this space, with very special administrative support and an early reading of this work, there is Diva Williams. Without a multigenerational look at one's own thoughts and work, there can be little reason to expect no validity or reliability (to use two scientific terms) to what we researchers put out there. On a line-by-line level also day-by-day, action-by-action, strategic context, the partnership of Meg Starr is more than even this writer can put into words. And though most of my life is lived both physically and intellectually—as well as my thoughts about organization—in an international context, my local collective Resistance in Brooklyn remains thoroughly grounding. I'll simply name two co-founding members specifically here: Betsy Mickel and Bob Lederer. I humbly dedicate this book to another founding RnBer, now past: Elspeth Meyer; her loss this last year, along with Sekou Odinga, Dylcia Pagan, and too many others, still stings; her practice helps provide a model of how to live a life well.